Three Plays
The Mayor of Zalamea
Life's a Dream
The Great Theatre of the World

The Mayor of Zalamea was first published by The Salamander Press, Edinburgh, in 1981 and in this edition by Absolute Press in 1990. Life's a Dream and The Great Theatre of the World were first published in 1990 by Absolute Press.

Produced and printed in England by WBC Print Ltd, Bristol.

ISBN 0 948230 26 6

The Mayor of Zalamea
Adapted by Adrian Mitchell

Life's a Dream
Adapted by Adrian Mitchell and John Barton

The Great Theatre of the World
Adapted by Adrian Mitchell

Three plays by
Pedro Calderón de la Barca

a b s o l u t e   c l a s s i c s

Contents

Introduction

Calderón de la Barca
or How I learned to stop worrying and love the Spanish Golden Age.

This introduction is not for scholars. They know far more about Calderon than I do. It is for those people who find themselves intimidated by the strangeness of Spain, even contemporary Spain, let alone the 17th Century Spain.

I felt that same nervousness only a few years ago. When I first read about the plays of the Spanish Golden Age – from around 1500 to 1681, the period in which Calderon, Lope de Vega, Cervantes, Tirso de Molina and Rojas Zorrilla flourished – I was dumbfounded by the system of values, especially the 'Honour' system which seemed to dominate the drama. It was only when I began to read the plays thoroughly that I discovered that you have to know very little about such matters to understand many of the greatest plays. Honour is such a strange word in England these days. Good name and reputation are still far easier to handle.

But when you read or act or watch "The Mayor of Zalamea" you need to know about human beings, not about social codes. Of course, the more you know about the social background the more you'll understand and enjoy. But most of us live in a world which doesn't allow time for historical research in between work or looking for work and going to the theatre. "The Mayor of Zalamea" was the first Spanish play I attempted, using a literal translation by Gwenda Pandolfi, sticking very closely to the text, using a kind of syllabic verse. This was commissioned by the National Theatre. When I read the play for the second time I knew that given a half-decent production, it must be popular. Michael Bogdanov's production was spare and strong and had at its centre a performance of pure gold by Michael Bryant. The production proved that there is no difficulty for an English audience with at least one of the Golden Age plays. It started at the Cottesloe and transferred to the Olivier because more seats were needed.

After its success the National suggested another Calderon, "Life's a Dream". But just as I was completing my version it was discovered that the Royal Shakespeare Company was about to stage a version of the same play by John Barton. I rang John, whom I didn't know at the time, to confirm that this was true, since the National had decided to scrap its plans. He is the most generous of bears and said something like: "Come on over and I'll show you mine and you show me yours". We both liked each other's versions. He'd solved problems I had been stumped by. I'd laid down some mean verse. John suggested mixing the versions together and that's what we did. He kept a kind of record of whose line was whose and it worked out about 46 per cent John, 46 per cent Adrian and eight per cent lines which were a mixture of the two. His production was highly acclaimed both in Stratford and London and once again the availability of Spanish drama to an English audience was proved.

"The Great Theatre of the World" was commissioned by the Mediaeval Players. The metaphor of the play, in which God is a theatre director and the World is his stage manager appealed to me strongly. So did the humour and the pathos and the poetic wonder of the play – it is a Christian play but a pretty undogmatic one, naturally, since Calderon could take it for granted that he had a Christian audience.

The theatre is a real world. This has advantages and disadvantages. One given factor for this production was that the Players have developed many circus skills like juggling and stilt-walking. We used this by giving the play an interlude half way through in which, since the play is much possessed by death, skeletons danced and played, giant skeletons walked on bone-like stilts and juggler skeletons demonstrated their art with skulls and bones. Disadvantages – the Players' grant couldn't stretch to a complete cast. One character, I was told, had to be left out. I chose the one which I felt was least relevant to a modern audience, the character Discretion, who chooses a contemplative life. Don't blame me, blame Mrs Thatcher. I suppose I could have written back Discretion into the play for this published edition. I decided not to. This is a version for Philistine Britain where even a very funny and affecting play about eternal truths has to lose, if not a limb, then a few fingers in the cause of cost-effectiveness. Calderon lived from 1600 to 1681. To find out about his life and work, read his entry in the Oxford Companion to Spanish Literature and Gerald Brenan's wonderful "The Literature of the Spanish People".

His work is sometimes characterised as formal, intellectual, spiritual, maybe somewhat cold. All these things are true, but there is far more to his plays. They're certainly not cold, they simply seem comparatively cool when you place them beside the red-hot passion of Lope de Vega. But there is a slow-burning passion in Calderon and also a lovely humour which is often forgotten. Lope de Vega (1562–1635) was surely a mixture of earth and fire. Calderon is air and water, a most beautiful fountain. And often, a fiery fountain.

ADRIAN MITCHELL

This collection is dedicated to all the theatre people involved in the first productions of these versions, with many thanks and much admiration.

The Mayor of Zalamea

(The Best Garrotting Ever Done)

This version of *The Mayor of Zalamea* was commissioned by the National Theatre and first performed at its Cottesloe Theatre on 17 July 1981 with the following cast:

Rebolledo, a soldier	Derek Newark
La Chispa, his mistress	Yvonne Bryceland
Sergeant, a veteran	Michael Beint
Captain Don Alvaro De Ataide	Daniel Massey
Don Mendo, an impoverished aristocrat	Daniel Thorndike
Nuno, his servant	Peter Løvstrøm
Pedro Crespo, a rich old farmer	Michael Bryant
Juan, his son	Clive Arrindell
Isabel, Pedro Crespo's daughter	Leslee Udwin
Ines, her cousin	Terry Diab
Don Lope De Figueroa, commander-in-chief	Basil Henson
Clerk	Nigel Bellairs
Philip II, King of Spain	Nicholas Selby
Soldiers and Farmers	Iain Rattray
	Glenn Williams
	Jane Evers
	Russell Kilmister
	Mark Ward
	Martin Garfield
	Stephen Hattersley
	Robert Oates
	Peter Løvstrøm

Director	Michael Bogdanov
Designer	Stephanie Howard
Lighting	Andrew Torble
Music	John White
Dance	Geraldine Stephenson
Fights	Malcolm Ransom
Voice	Jenny Patrick
Production Manager	Jason Barnes
Stage Manager	Howard Kingston
Assistant Stage Managers	Michael Roberts
	Tony Godel
	Cathie Coulsen
Sound	Rick Clarke
Assistant Production Manager	Tiggi Trethowan
Publicist	Mary Parsons

This adaptation is based on a literal translation by Gwenda Pandolfi.

Notes

Scenes

Scene endings are indicated by the symbol ◇ rather than formal divisions, since the action of the original would have been more or less continuous. But clearly the contrast in the second act between the serene, ordered beauty of Crespo's walled garden and the dark chaos of the forest calls for more than a bare stage.

Title

The original title was *The Best Garrotting Ever Done*. In the 19th Century this was changed to *The Mayor of Zalamea* as a reflection of more refined taste. I like both titles.

Syllabics

Most of the lines are of eight syllables with varied metre. But I've used my ear rather than my fingers for counting. So the word 'mayor' for instance would sometimes count as two syllables, sometimes as one – depending on how it would be pronounced in the sentence.
Line endings should normally be ignored.

Characters

Crespo's ideas of honour and good name are not the conventional ones, but come from his heart. His humbling of himself before the Captain is an action of Christ-like implications.
Juan is callow and his concept of honour is a conventional one. He's also confused and hot-headed – he can pity his sister in one breath and in the next declare that she must die. Don Lope's great loyalty is to the army and his brother officers.
The Captain is an aristocrat as well as an officer. The Sergeant is an old soldier, not a ruffian like Rebolledo.
Don Mendo is an impoverished aristocrat.

Verse

Four main verse forms are used by Calderon and these are followed in this version. They are:
1. Lines of eight syllables rhyming abba cddc.
2. Lines of eight syllables with alternative lines ending in an assonance or half-rhyme – abacdedf.
3. Rhyming couplets with lines of unequal length.
4. Five lines of eight syllables rhyming ababa or abaab or aabba or abbab or aabab.

The metre is varied throughout.

Act One
The Road Leading to Zalamea
A Street in Zalamea
The Street in Front of Pedro Crespo's House

Act Two
The Street and Walled Garden Behind Pedro Crespo's House
The Forest Outside Zalamea
The Street in Front of Pedro Crespo's House
The Forest

Act Three
The Forest
The Street in Front of Pedro Crespo's House
The Captain's Lodgings
A Room in Pedro Crespo's House
Outside The Prison

Act One

[*The Road Leading to Zalamea.* SOLDIERS *marching. Among them* REBOLLEDO *and his mistress* LA CHISPA.]

Rebolledo	Left! Right! And to hell with the rat Marches us here and there and back, Nowhere to no-place with a pack And with no booze –
All	– Amen to that.
Rebolledo	Are we only rag-tag bleeders? Raddled tramps with gypsy manners Trudging behind dusty banners, Grateful there's a band to lead us And the great drum –
1st Soldier	– For Jesus' sake!
Rebolledo	And the great drum for once keeps mum, And the great drum for once is dumb, So that our heads, for once, don't ache?
2nd Soldier	Don't let the bastards grind you down. We're all shagged out, and underfed. But soon we'll have a feather bed And some grub in a friendly town.
Rebolledo	Friendly or not, what if I'm dead? Or, if I manage to survive, God alone knows if I'll arrive To find myself well-billeted. Towns are all scared stiff of pillage. Up speaks your old City Father: "Awfully sorry, but we'd rather Pass you on to the next village." "Right", says our crafty Commander To the revered City Father: "We can slog on if you'd rather – For a substantial back-hander." Then the Commander comes striding Back to the ranks: "I've an order – We march ten miles to the border." We march – that bugger is riding.

God above – to you I'm talking:
If we get to Zalamea
And they try, by force or prayer,
To persuade us to keep walking,
They will take their day excursion
Minus me, for I'll have scurried
Out of sight. NO I'm not worried,
It won't be my first desertion.

1st Soldier   I know – and you won't be the first
Who hung for not giving two hoots.
The old man's as tough as old boots.
All generals are shits – he's the worst.
Don Lope de Figueroa
May be a heroic old fart
But his tongue's black and so's his heart.
Even Satan stoops no lower.
Don Lope, with that twisted smile,
Would send the closest friend he's got
Off to the axe or the garrotte
Without the bother of a trial.

Rebolledo   Look – if you want to know what's what –
Just hang about and watch my style.

2nd Soldier   You're a deserter, and you boast?

Rebolledo   If I'm concerned – death makes me laugh –
It's only on this girl's behalf.
She follows me from post to post.

Chispa   Senor Rebolledo, you fail
To understand. Let your fears fly,
For it's notorious that I
Can bear as much as any male
And your concern dishonours me,
For, if I serve you sir, I know
I shall expect to undergo
Thousands of hardships honourably.
Were I genteel, I'd not be yours
But live in luxury and state
With some wealthy magistrate
And never step outdoors.
I'm not genteel. I've teeth. I've claws,
And I've decided that I'll go

To hell for you, Rebolledo
And without grumbling. Why? I'm yours.
Don't fear for me. Just hope for us.

Rebolledo   Praise God! I see, who once was blind.
– The flower of all womankind!

Chispa   [*Sings*]
I am
Diddle diddle dylans
Queen of
All the bloody villains.

Rebolledo   [*Sings*]
I am
Diddle diddle dumpets
King of
All the bloody strumpets.

Chispa   [*Sings*]
Generals slaughtering all over Europe
Admirals battling on every sea.

Rebolledo   [*Sings*]
Somebody else go and kill the Moroccans
They never done any harm to me.

Chispa   [*Sings*]
Pat-a-cake baker's man fill up my oven
I can eat anything you can bake.

Rebolledo   [*Sings*]
Pat-a-bull butcher's wife kill me a chicken
Mutton and pork give me stomach ache.

1st Soldier   Silver larks through clouds ascending,
Showering earth with harmonies,
Please accept my apologies
Shut your gobs – our journey's ending.
Here's the troops – you lucky people!
There's the church-spire! Who's for prayer?

Rebolledo   Sure this town is Zalamea?

Chispa   That's the Zalamea steeple.
Let the bells go bloody ding-dong.
As we end our little sing-song
Down there, we'll make the rafters ring

A thousand times a week, for I'm
A bird whose food is tune and rhyme.
When other women weep – I sing.
I sing too much . . . my only fault.

Rebolledo   Until the Sergeant bothers to
Strut up and tell us what to do
Why don't we shamble to a halt?
We don't know how to enter town,
Marching in ranks or –

1st Soldier   – Shut up you.
What's to be done we'll soon be told.
Here comes the Sergeant, and behold
Here comes the Captain, right on cue.

Captain   Congratulate me gentlemen!
I invite you all to stay a
Day or two in Zalamea.
Yes, we're billeted! Till when?
Until our General and his force
Can join us from Llarena, and
Don Lope then assumes command.
He'll be here soon enough. Of course
You're all dog tired. Marched a long way.
Well, make yourselves at home. Right here.

Rebolledo   Well sir, I think you earned a cheer.

All   The Captain! Hip, hip, hip hooray!

Captain   Your billets have all been assigned.
Office of Accommodation
Has more detailed information.

Chispa   I've a weird problem on my mind.
Like a clock it goes on ticking –
What's it <u>mean</u> for heaven's sake:
"Pat-a-bull butcher's wife kill me a chicken,
Mutton and pork give me stomach ache"?

[*Exeunt*]

◇

[*A street in Zalamea. Enter* CAPTAIN *and* SERGEANT, *meeting*]

Captain	Sergeant!
Sergeant	Sir!
Captain	Lodgings. What's the news? You said you'd inspect my billet.
Sergeant	Done sir.
Captain	Good man. Tell me, will it Have decent bedding, food and booze?
Sergeant	It should, sir, for the owner's rich – A peasant farmer, but they say the Proudest man in Zalamea. An arrogant son-of-a-bitch, Born in a barn, but got such side You'd think he'd traced his lineage Back to the Mesolithic age.
Captain	Rich? He's entitled to some pride. So, it's a farmhouse where I'll stay?
Sergeant	Mansion, sir. The epitome Of all your quarters ought to be. Palatial, sir. But I should say I did not pick this Xanadhu For architecture, but because A lady lives behind its doors, A really beautiful young –
Captain	– Who?
Sergeant	His daughter, sir.
Captain	A pig's a pig. Sergeant, a girl who's peasant-born May be vain, but she's peasant-spawn – Malformed red hands and feet too big.
Sergeant	You're a minority of one.
Captain	I'm wrong?
Sergeant	No sir, let's say that I'm Sure there's no way of killing time Better than – doing it for fun, With no love guff. A patch of grass,

A bottle and a loaf or two
And a ripe peasant princess who
Can't tell her elbow from her arse.

Captain   Rustic frolicking's a sport
For oafs. To arouse my passion
She must be dressed in the fashion,
Elegant enough for the court –
Otherwise I couldn't lower
My high standards to the sewer.

Sergeant   Personally, sir, I'd screw her
If I thought she was a goer.
If you won't, I will. Let's inspect
These digs, then get dug in. Let's go.

Captain   Sergeant, I think you ought to know
Your attitude is incorrect,
For, when a man is passion-swayed
And sees his loved one walking by
He says "My Lady" with a sigh.
He does not say "My dairy-maid".
Ladies are, for the man of taste,
Artistic objects to acquire.
One peasant piece – and his entire
Collection is at once debased.
But what's that clatter?

Sergeant   It's some bloke
Fell off a horse's skeleton,
A Rosinante type of mount.
The rider too, he's skin and bone
Like Don Quixote in the book
Cervantes authored. A somewhat
Impoverished pretentious knight.

Captain   Looks like something of a dimwit.

Sergeant   Time to move, sir. Don't you reckon?

Captain   Absolutely. Here's your mission.
Take my kit to my lodgings. Then
Bring me fuller information.

[*Exeunt*]

◇

[*Outside Pedro Crespo's House. Enter* DON MENDO, *an impoverished aristocrat, with his undernourished servant* NUNO.]

Don Mendo	How fares my steed?
Nuno	Flat on his back. Hasn't the strength to raise a smile.
Don Mendo	Perhaps he requires exercise.
Nuno	No, he requires a decent meal.
Don Mendo	A good gallop would refresh him.
Nuno	Fodder would be even better.
Don Mendo	Have you unleashed my greyhounds yet?
Nuno	Wait until I've warned the butcher.
Don Mendo	I must show that I've dined richly. Nuno! My toothpick! No, the gold one.
Nuno	Sorry sir, we traded that one For that rabbit from those children.
Don Mendo	If there's one man in all Europe Who maintains I've had no dinner, I will challenge him to fight And with arms maintain my honour.
Nuno	Isn't it fairer to maintain Your humble servant?
Don Mendo	Sir, you jest. Inform me: have militia Descended on this township?
Nuno	Yes.
Don Mendo	Now my compassion fountains up For the poor, whose skimpy rations Will be purloined.
Nuno	I'm sorry for Those who have no expectations.
Don Mendo	For whom, rogue?
Nuno	The Nobility. The soldiers of our great nation –

	Where would they be if nobles had To feed and water them?
Don Mendo	Tell me.
Nuno	They'd be dead of malnutrition.
Don Mendo	Rest.in peace, father! You mock him When you mock aristocracy. Respected father, you left me A patent of nobility, Illuminated blue and gold – Blue blood, gold crowns, you see. My flesh Is thus certified thoroughbred.
Nuno	Father, I'd rather you'd left cash.
Don Mendo	I was exclusively conceived. But I can't be over-grateful To my father for begetting Me, Don Mendo, as a noble. Had he not been highly born I'd have forced him to forbear And refused to fertilise That rich egg which my mother bore.
Nuno	That would have been a fancy trick.
Don Mendo	No, elementary etiquette.
Nuno	But I don't know –
Don Mendo	– But how could you Know what is meet and what's not meet?
Nuno	What's meat? A faintish memory . . . Of what? Some fragrant, chewable, Pink substance? No, I can't recall . . . Such words as cheese – trout – pineapple, Paella, brandy, turkey, ham, Sausage, sardines, sherry, shellfish – Names of old friends I've not seen since I thought meet to do you service.
Don Mendo	When I say meet, I don't mean meat But meet. Still, food is relevant Since my embryo was composed Of food eaten by my parents.

Nuno	Your parents ate? Well, that's a trait You've not inherited, my lord.
Don Mendo	This food, this fuel, is transformed Into the baby's flesh and blood. Thus, had my father just consumed Ignoble garlic, my fine flared Nostrils had warned my brain and I Would have cried out: "Dismount! How dare You stir a dish of filigree Silver with a wooden ladle!"
Nuno	It's true then, is it, sir?
Don Mendo	What's true?
Nuno	Hunger pains cause the brains to addle.
Don Mendo	Buffoon, do you say I'm raving?
Nuno	No, ravenous. A lesser man Would have been starving, for the time Is nearly three – mid-afternoon. Our mouths, all day, have been empty But for saliva, tongues and teeth.
Don Mendo	What has the time to do with me? I'll teach you an essential truth: Men are unequally designed. Farmhands gulp their slops with passion. Merchants dine with finer manners. Noblemen need no nutrition.
Nuno	Wish someone would ennoble me.
Don Mendo	Enough of sordid matters – we Are entering the street in which Isabel dwells.
Nuno	But tell me why, If you're so passionately fond Of Isabel, why don't you go And ask her father for her hand? That way her father'd meet your needs – Banquets galore, booze in abundance – While you, as fair exchange, could give Your blue blood to his descendants.

Don Mendo	Silence. My financial standing Is not so low that I will stoop To plead for marriage with a girl Born of a commoner –
Nuno	– Hey, stop. If you don't want to marry her What are you doing wooing her?
Don Mendo	I seek no ceremony, just A mad affair, and when I tire Of Isabel, a nunnery Would seem appropriate for her. Now, is she visible? You look.
Nuno	If Pedro Crespo sees me here I'm scared –
Don Mendo	– You are my serving man. You serve me. I protect you. What On earth is there to fear?
Nuno	Nothing. At least I don't fear getting fat.
Don Mendo	Servants today! How typical! Such feebleness! Such gluttony!
Nuno	With her cousin Ines she is Standing up on that balcony.
Don Mendo	Tell her this: over the beauteous Horizon of her balcony Rises a second sun, herself, Diamond-crowned at five to three.

[ISABEL *and her cousin* INES, *are seen on the balcony*]

Ines	Isabel, come and stand by me. Let's watch the military parade Marching through Zalamea.
Isabel	No. You know I'd rather stay inside While Don Mendo's lurking out there. Seeing him always angers me.
Ines	But Don Mendo takes such endless Trouble to court you gallantly.

Isabel	Wish he'd take his trouble elsewhere.
Ines	Don't be so hard, for heaven's sake.
Isabel	Well, how am I supposed to feel? How should I treat him?
Ines	As a joke.
Isabel	The joke is stale. My laughter's dead.
Don Mendo	Until now – I will take a bold Breath and swear by my noble name – Of all oaths most unbreakable – Till now the sun had failed to rise. It is no wonder she disdains To do so till your blush is seen, And then she condescends, and dawns.
Isabel	I've tried to tell you many times, Senor Mendo, it's all useless. Your public vows embarrass me. All your hopes of love are baseless. Every day outside my front door Like a sentry you're positioned.
Don Mendo	If lovely women only knew How much, when they are impassioned Their loveliness increases – why They'd use, not rouge, but high disdain. You are so gorgeous, by my life! Hit me again, again, again!
Isabel	Sir, if my words have that effect, I'll drop the curtain on this farce. Ines, dear cousin, will you slam The shutters in Don Mendo's face?

[*Exit* ISABEL]

Ines	Illustrious knight, husband to be Of somebody – please God not me, I don't think you could use a wife. You need a good free meal. Push off.

[*Exit* INES]

Don Mendo	Great beauties have a destiny – This choice: to love or not to love.

Nuno	But we've a noble's destiny – To be rejected and to starve.

[*Enter* PEDRO CRESPO, *rich farmer*]

Crespo	Whenever I come in or out I see that lanky layabout Sighing and trudging up and down Like an old boar without a sow.
Nuno	Look out. Here comes Pedro Crespo.
Don Mendo	Her father – he'll suspect that I'm Here for some dubious purpose.

[*Enter* JUAN, PEDRO CRESPO's *son*]

Juan	[*Aside*] Whenever I come home I find This numbskull leaning at my door, With rich rags and false dignity.
Nuno	[*To* DON MENDO] Old Crespo's son is coming now.
Don Mendo	[*To* NUNO] Act more sophisticatedly.
Crespo	[*Aside*] Oh. My son Juan is approaching.
Juan	[*Aside*] Oh my God. My father's coming.
Don Mendo	[*To* NUNO] Bluff it out. [*To* CRESPO] Oh, Pedro Crespo, How's farming?
Crespo	Fine. How's loitering?

[*Exeunt* DON MENDO *and* NUNO]

	Every time he bothers me, I'll give him double bother back.
Juan	Oh God! That old fool gets me riled – Father, are you just home from work?
Crespo	I've been down at the threshing floor, Yes, overseeing the farmhands. The heaps of corn grow steadily

To form enormous, burnished mounds.
I watched them from a hundred yards –
A shining, soaring mountain range
Of gold, the finest, purest gold,
By heaven perfectly displayed
Against the pure blue of the sky.
Winnowing forks beat rhythmically
Allowing the swift-sifting winds
To puff the chaff out of the way
Leaving a pyramid of grain.
(Chaff shows the deference to grain
Farmers are meant to show to Lords).
Oh, my dear Lord, please give me time
To shift your bounteous gift indoors
Before you rot it with your rain
Or scatter it with your whirlwind.
And what have you been doing, Juan?

Juan I can't tell you what's on my mind
Without infuriating you.
This afternoon I went to play
Pelota. Two games. I lost both.

Crespo What's wrong? Provided that you paid.

Juan Father, I didn't pay, because
I didn't have the cash. So I
Thought that I'd ask you if I could –

Crespo Now listen. Time for good advice.
Two things that you should never do.
Don't promise the impossible
And never play for higher stakes
Than you can plonk on the table.
This way you may lose all your cash
But not lose your reputation.

Juan Your advice is just like you, sir –
Simple. I accept your caution
And pay you back with this advice;
When a man asks for your small change
Don't tell him how to change his life.

Crespo All right, son, you've had your revenge.

[*Enter* SERGEANT]

Sergeant   Old Crespo's mansion? Is that right?

Crespo   Yes it is. What are your orders?

Sergeant   Move in quick and dump the gear of
                   Don Alvaro de Ataide.
                   He's our company commander,
                   Captain of the mob that's stationed
                   At Zalamea as from now.

Crespo   All right. You are welcome sergeant.
                   My house and farm are for the use
                   Of God, the King and the King's men.
                   Leave his kit here, it's safe while we
                   Prepare a room for your Captain.
                   Say I await him, say my house
                   Is his and everything in it.
                   He can arrive at any time.

Sergeant   He'll be along in a few minutes.

                   [*Exit* SERGEANT]

Juan   Father, you're rich. How can you let
                   The army overrun your house?

Crespo   I am compelled to, for the law
                   Says no exemptions are allowed.

Juan   Except the nobles. Why not buy
                   A patent of nobility?

Crespo   Name me one man who doesn't know
                   I'm from a peasant family.
                   Nobody. Right. So if I buy
                   Such a certificate, who's gained?
                   The King – he gets the patent fee.
                   You can't buy blue blood by the pint.
                   Would folk say: Pedro Crespo's changed –
                   The peasant has become a prince?
                   They'd say: he tried to buy respect –
                   It cost six thousand silver coins.
                   I've lots of money, and that proves
                   I'm rich, not that I'm honourable.
                   Listen, this may seem trivial,
                   But it's not a bad example.
                   There's this bald man, been bald for years,

Totally bald – one day he goes
And buys himself a sudden wig.
Do people think he's hairy? No.
What do they say when he walks by?
"There goes old Pedro in his wig."
His dome's invisible, but they
All know he's bald as any egg.

Juan

Wearing a wig might save him from
Some problems. It might ease his mind.
Besides, it would act as a thatch
Against the sun and frost and wind.

Crespo

I want no honour that's unreal.
My parents and their parents were
Ordin'ry people. So are we.
Now call your sister.

Juan

                         She is here.

[*Enter* ISABEL *and* INES]

Crespo

Daughter, great Philip, King of Spain –
God, may he reign a thousand years –
Marches to Lisbon to be crowned
Rightful lord of the Portuguese.
Because of this the roads are jammed
– Guns, horses, siege machinery.
Our Flanders force is coming home
Led by the fearsome Don Lope.
Today some soldiers come to lodge
Here in our house. What must be done?
You must move to the attic rooms.
Stay out of sight until they've gone.

Isabel

I'd come to ask you if I might
Move up there. Thank you. Otherwise
Ines and I would have to hear
Endless male stupidities.
We'll perch up there together and
Tell no one, not the sun himself
Who thinks that he knows everything.

Crespo

Good girl. Away you go. God bless.

Isabel

Ines, come on.

Ines	Yes, Isabel.

Isn't that typically mannish?
Any excitement – we vanish!
It's all right, we're going
And taking our sewing.

[*Exeunt* ISABEL, INES *and* CRESPO]

[*Enter* CAPTAIN *and* SERGEANT]

Sergeant   This, sir, is where you're billeted.

Captain   All right. Unpack my kit and make my bed.

Sergeant   Right away. [*Aside*] His orders suit me.
I'll get an eyeful of this famous beauty.

[*Exit* SERGEANT]

Juan   Welcome. I'm greatly honoured, sir
To greet you as a gentleman and officer.
[*Aside*]
He stands there like a god, potent but bored.
I wish I had that style, that uniform, that sword.

Captain   Happy to be here. Decent place you've got.

Juan   Captain, forgive us if your dinner's not
Quite ready. Father ordered everything
Should be the same as we would serve the king.
Now he's conferring with the cook.
I'd better go and have a look
To make sure all the men are standing by, sir.

Captain   Thank you, young man.

Juan   Your servant till I die, sir.

[*Exit* JUAN. *Enter* SERGEANT]

Captain   Sergeant, have you tracked down this hot
Young Crespo daughter?

Sergeant   I have not!
I searched the bedrooms, kitchen, underneath the stair,
The cupboards, barns and stables and nowhere
Is there a single trace of virgin, sir.

Captain   Bloody old peasant must have hidden her,
Jealous old –

Sergeant	– May I say a word? I found a maid, who says the bird Is locked up in an attic room for fear Of all the randy military down here. She's under orders never to be seen.
Captain	Why are all peasants so insanely mean? If I'd run into her today I'd not have thrown a second glance her way. But, just because the old boy keeps her hidden – It's irresistible – fruit that's forbidden – I'm going up to see her.
Sergeant	– Now There's just the tactics aspect – how? You can't say: Where's your daughter? Kiss me quick.
Captain	I've got to see her. Let's work out a trick.
Sergeant	The simplest plan is always best – Climb up the tree and grab the nest.
Captain	Sergeant. I've got a great idea. You pretend – no, this soldier here, He's a bit quicker, he's the man To help me with my master plan.

[*Enter* REBOLLEDO *and* CHISPA]

Rebolledo	The Captain! Here's a chance for me To nobble him –
Chispa	Talk sensibly. Try not to seem too wild and dense.
Rebolledo	Oh goddess, give me your intelligence.
Chispa	I'll give you something you could do without – That's all you give me –
Rebolledo	– Hang about . . . Grant me a favour? You can.
Captain	I'll try. You seem the sort of man I like. You're spirited and smart.
Sergeant	He's a brave soldier, sir. And so's his tart.
Captain	You're glum. Why, Rebolledo?

Rebolledo	I am sad Because I've lost all that I have, have had And ever shall have, an immense Loss in the present, past and future tense. I'm broke. Captain, you can help me Officially but unofficially.
Captain	Two reasons and I'll favour you not once, but twice.
Rebolledo	Make me the officer in charge of cards and dice. My reasons: I'm in debt, no joke. My other reason . . . I'm an honest bloke?
Captain	You're a persuasive chap. All right. You're gambling officer as from tonight.
Chispa	The Captain's smiling. That'll be the day When I'm the mistress of a croupier.
Rebolledo	I'm overwhelmed –
Captain	– Before you start Your business, there's a secret in my heart I'd like to trust you with. You can Help me with an ingenious plan.
Rebolledo	The quicker they grow the quicker they do it, Tell me the plot and we'll go to it.
Captain	I want to go upstairs . . .
Rebolledo	. . . Why so dramatic?
Captain	There is a person hiding in the attic, A woman whom I long to see.
Rebolledo	What is she hiding from?
Captain	From me.
Rebolledo	Why not nip up?
Captain	For conversation? My act must have some explanation, Some pretext. All right, we'll pretend To quarrel fiercely. Then my friend, You run away, screaming, upstairs. Sword drawn, I follow, take you unawares, And chase you, with ferocious strides, Into the room where the girl hides.

Rebolledo	Yes, sir.
Chispa	Seeing them talk that way – I'm sure I'll soon be mistress of a croupier.
Rebolledo	[*Pretending to be angry*] God's teeth but there's no justice! They Give <u>you</u> a hand-out any time you say But I get nothing. That's because I'm straight But you're as bent as an old fig-tree, mate. Funny – a chicken's heart inside a rat.
Chispa	He's gone berserk.
Captain	Don't talk to me like that.
Rebolledo	I'm right. So I've the right to put you right, All right?
Captain	All wrong – shut up, you parasite Or you'll soon be a corpse, with fleas on.
Rebolledo	You're still my Captain, that's the only reason I'll shut my gob. But if I'd got My commission I'd –
Captain	[*Grasping his sword*] – You'd what?
Chispa	Don't sir. [*Aside*] I think he's going to die.
Rebolledo	Don't give me that.
Captain	I can't imagine why I haven't crushed this vile insect. [*Draws his sword*]
Rebolledo	[*Fleeing*] Well, I retire, but only from respect For that insignia of rank –
Captain	– See how He runs. See how I kill –
Chispa	– He's had it now.
Sergeant	Hang on, sir.
Chispa	Please, sir.
Sergeant	Put your sword away.

Chispa	I'll never be the mistress of a croupier.

[CAPTAIN *exits, waving his sword, in pursuit of* REBOLLEDO. *Enter* JUAN, *with a sword, and* PEDRO CRESPO]

Chispa	Help, everybody! An emergency!
Crespo	What's happened?
Juan	What's the urgency?
Chispa	The Captain, with a sword, began to chase A soldier who'd called him fig-face. Then they whizzed up that flight of stairs. They're mad.
Crespo	That's the worst luck I ever had.
Chispa	Go stop them.
Juan	[*Aside*] I knew very well There was no point in hiding Isabel.

[*Exeunt* CRESPO *and* JUAN *up the stairs*]

◇

[*The attic stairs of Pedro Crespo's house.* REBOLLEDO *enters, fleeing, to confront* ISABEL *and* INES.]

Rebolledo	Ladies, excuse me, but you know That shrines are always sanctuaries? So please grant me sanctuary In this shrine to Aphrodite.
Isabel	Who's forcing you to hide like this?
Ines	Were you chased here by some villain?
Isabel	Who is this enemy of yours?

[*Enter* CAPTAIN *and* SERGEANT]

Captain	I am. Now I have to kill him For I've sworn by the living God To cut his throat because he –
Isabel	– Please Swallow your anger. Sheathe your sword. He sought protection in my room.

I guard him. You're a gentleman.
So you'll respect my wishes, sir,
Officers respect all women.

Captain   In any other sanctuary
By now he'd be past all caring,
But your beauty stays my sword-arm.
For your beauty's sake, I spare him.
But tell me, lady, is it fair
To stop me killing, righteously,
While your voice, eyes, hair, mouth and form
Have all conspired to murder me?

Isabel   Sir, all our lives we'll be obliged
That you have been so courteous.
Now kindly let this soldier go
And expect nothing else from us.

Captain   Not only is your loveliness
Of a perfection rarely found
But it forms a warm alliance
With perfect clarity of mind.

[*Enter* PEDRO CRESPO *and* JUAN, *with swords drawn*]

Crespo   What is this, sir? What's happening?
I ran up here because I feared
I'd find you killing someone but
Instead I find you –

Isabel   – Oh dear Lord.

Crespo   – Courting a woman. Is that right?
Wonderful how your anger burns
Up like a furnace and then out
Just like a candle.

Captain   I was born
With a strong sense of duty. So
Out of respect for ladies, I
Banked down my fury, as you see.

Crespo   Isabel is my daughter, sir.
A peasant girl of peasant stock
And not a lady –

Juan   [*Aside*]
– Jesus Christ!

Now I see – it's all been a trick
To get him into the attic.
Yes. He never would have stabbed him.
It's sickening. I'll stop it now –
They're laughing at me. [*To* CAPTAIN] Well, Captain,
If you'd bothered to look down
From your great height you would have seen
My father, eager to serve you.
You treat him most contemptuously.

Crespo   Who asked you to interfere, boy?
Who's shown contempt for anyone?
Tell me why the Captain shouldn't
Pursue a soldier if the man
Has angered him. My Isabel
Appreciates his courtesy
In sparing her by sparing him.
There's nothing wrong that I can see.

Captain   I acted most straightforwardly.
Boy, you had better watch your tongue.

Juan   I'm watching very carefully.

Crespo   Don't you dare to be insulting.

Captain   Since you're present, sir, I'll not
Chastise your insolent young son.

Crespo   No, Captain, you will not, because
His beatings come from me alone.

Juan   Punishment I'll take from my father –
But I won't from any other.

Captain   What would you do to stop me then?

Juan   Stake my life upon my honour.

Captain   What honour can a peasant have?

Juan   The same as you. Captain, hasn't
Anyone told you there'd be no
Captains if there were no peasants.
But peasants could live happily,
If all captains ceased to exist.

Captain   By God's name, now I'll slaughter you.

Crespo   You'll have to reckon with me first

[*They draw their swords*]

Rebolledo   For Christ's sake, Chispa, don't stand there,
This fight is genuine. Let's go.

Chispa   Guards! Send the Guards!

Rebolledo   Don Lope's here!
Our General approaches.

Captain   No!

[*Enter* DON LOPE, *the old general, wearing a cloak bearing the
insignia of an order of knighthood. He has a bad leg.*]

Don Lope   What's up then? Must the first damn thing
To greet me on my arrival
Be one of my damned officers
Sword-dancing in some damn garret?

Captain   [*Aside*]
Of all the moments in my life
Don Lope had to choose this one.

Crespo   [*Aside*]
You see that, God? That son of mine
Was managing to hold his own.

Don Lope   Damn all of you! What's going on?
Tell me now, or by God, I swear
I'll take each man and woman here
And boot them, damn it, down the stairs.
I climb up here, despite my gout,
About which you don't give a damn,
To find a band of maniacs
Who, when I question them, go dumb.
Tell me some damn-fool story, please.

Crespo   Nothing that matters happened, sir.

Don Lope   Somehow I'd rather know the truth.

Captain   Sir, I was ordered to stay here.
When I arrived, this –

Don Lope   – Please go on.

Captain   – This man insulted my good name.
Naturally I drew. He fled.
I followed him up to this room.

	I found him with these peasant girls.
	Then their father and brother
	Started screaming bloody murder.

Don Lope   You're all damn lucky I arrived.
                All right, where's the insulting man
                Whose insolence sparked off this brawl?

Rebolledo   [*Aside*]
                I'm carrying the can again.

Isabel   This is the man who ran away
                And hid here.

Don Lope   [*Laconically sentencing him*]
                                    Two drops on the rope.

Rebolledo   What sir?

Don Lope   Hands tied behind your back.
                You're hauled up, then allowed to drop.

Rebolledo   I think that's most unsuitable.

Chispa   [*Aside*]
                This time they'll cripple him for good.

Captain   Oh Rebolledo! For God's sake . . .
                I'll get you off — don't say a word.

Rebolledo   Don't say a word? Don't make me laugh.
                If I'm silent I'll be carted
                Off to some tree where I shall be
                Seriously dislocated.
                — Sir, the Captain ordered me to
                Fake a quarrel, for he said his
                Plan was to chase me up the stairs
                And break in here to meet these ladies.

Crespo   You see, sir, we were in the right.

Don Lope   Wrong, sir. If you'd killed the Captain
                Zalamea would have paid.
                Every house and farm and tavern
                Would be carefully destroyed —
                That's the custom. Call the drummer.
                Tell him to announce this order:
                Every soldier to his billet.
                Nobody to leave his quarters.

A soldier who's found out of doors
Dies. That applies all day today.

[*To* CAPTAIN]
Now, so you'll drop this scheme of yours

[*To* CRESPO]
And so your grievances can fade,
The Captain will lodge somewhere else
For damn it, I'll stay here. Not long –
Just till I leave for Guadalupe
To lead the army of the King.

Captain   Your wishes are completely clear.
I'll obey them to the letter.

[*Exeunt* CAPTAIN, SOLDIERS, REBOLLEDO *and* CHISPA]

Crespo   [*To* DON LOPE]
Come with me.

[CRESPO *and* DON LOPE *leave the attic and walk downstairs together.*]

                           I want to express
All my gratitude to you, sir.
You saved me when I surely ran
The risk of ruining myself.

Don Lope   What do you mean, man? How could you
Bring ruin on yourself yourself?

Crespo   By murdering a man who tried
To insult me by act and word.

Don Lope   Are you aware, God damn it, that
The man's a Captain?

Crespo   Yes, by God!
But if he was a General
And tried to damage my good name
I'd kill him.

Don Lope   Any man who tries
To even touch the uniform
Of my lousiest drummer-boy –
Damn him, I'll hang him joyfully.

Crespo   The man who slanders my good name –
Damn him, I'll hang him just as high.

Don Lope	Socially speaking, you accept All sorts of impositions – no?
Crespo	Upon my house and money – yes – Upon my reputation – no. I'll give up life and property At the King's word. But honour is The offspring of the soul of man. And the soul, God tells us, is his.
Don Lope	By Christ, Crespo, it starts to look As if you might be in the right.
Crespo	Don Lope, here's the reason why – I've not been in the wrong, by Christ!
Don Lope	Travelling – I'm exhausted. And so's my infernal leg.
Crespo	Why not have a good night's rest In an infernal feather bed?
Don Lope	Hellfire! Is the damn bed made?
Crespo	Yes.
Don Lope	Right, I'll unmake it.
Crespo	So, to bed.
Don Lope	[*Aside*] What an obstinate old peasant. Something of a crackpot, I'd say.
Crespo	[*Aside*] He's a hard man, this Don Lope. Damn it, he won't see things my way.

[*End of Act One*]

Act Two

[*The street behind Pedro Crespo's house. A walled garden lies
between the street and the house. It is dusk.* DON MENDO *and his
manservant* NUNO *enter the street.*]

Don Mendo This information – who's it from?

Nuno Ginesa – she's the lady's maid.

Don Mendo The Captain has, during a fight,
Whether real or simulated,
Been captivated by a glimpse
Of my lady?

Nuno So much so
That he takes no breakfast, lunch or
Dinner either – just like you, sir.
All day the Captain lurks around
Her doorstep and will not be moved.
And an old servant doggedly
Delivers messages of love
Each hour upon the hour –

Don Mendo – Enough!
You pour a generous overdose
Of deadly nightshade down the throat
Of my devastated soul – cease!

Nuno Such medicine should never be
Taken on an empty stomach.

Don Mendo Fool, be serious. I find your
Gluttonous wise-cracks aren't comic.

Nuno That's because my belly's tragic.

Don Mendo What answer does my lady send
The Captain?

Nuno Same as she sends you.
Isabel, like a goddess, lives
Beyond the range of the profane
Prayers of mortals down below.

Don Mendo God damn it! Bring me better news!

[DON MENDO *slaps* NUNO's *face*]

Nuno   May all your wisdom teeth explode! You
Bust a couple of my gnashers.
Don't worry. They were unemployed.
My gums can cope with my rations.
The Captain's coming –

Don Mendo   – By God's teeth
Now I'd assassinate him – but
Isabel would be compromised.

Nuno   Well, she'd survive. But you might not.

[*Enter the* CAPTAIN, SERGEANT *and* REBOLLEDO]

Don Mendo   I'll camouflage myself so I
Can overhear what they're saying.

Captain   This fire I feel is not mere love –
A mere theme for versifying.
No. An obsession, bulged with rage.
Anger beats through my blood. Like steel
My skin and muscles are drawn tense.

Rebolledo   Pity you ever saw that kid.
Remember she's a peasant, sir,
And don't let her beauty fool you.

Captain   What message did her servant bring?

Rebolledo   Do I really have to tell you?

Don Mendo   [*To* NUNO]
What must be, must be. Now that night
Drops her skirts over this section,
Before my instinct to survive
Has dissolved my will to action,
Bring me my sword and dagger –

Nuno   – Sir,
As for weapons, you can take a
Choice between a carving-knife, a
Broom, a hammer and a poker.

Don Mendo   You will endeavour to procure
Equipment for this enterprise
Immediately –

Nuno
                              – Let's move along
Before the Captain notices.

[*Exit* DON MENDO *and* NUNO]

Captain
A peasant girl, but she displays
Aristocratic haughtiness.
I offer passion – she replies
With cold-blooded unfriendliness.

Sergeant
It's like this: your peasant girl, sir,
Is leery of your officer.
Your local yokel's got more chance –
He spends five years in courting her.
Ask yourself: Are you being fair?
You may move on tomorrow, why
Should a young lady hear you out
And come across, all in one day?

Captain
All in one day the sun whirls up,
Lights the world, drops into the dark.
All in one day, kingdoms change hands,
Palaces are crushed into dust.
All in one day a city's lost
And gloating victors flood its streets.
All in one day the ocean may
Be level and tumultuous.
All in one day, a man is born.
All in one day, a man must die.
And so, all in one day, my love
May view the darkness and the light
As planets do. All in one day,
My love may rise, my love may fall,
Like an empire. All in one day,
My love may harbour animals,
Like a wood people wander through.
Tame and angry – like the ocean.
Glorious, ruinous – like war.
Love's mastered my passions and mind,
My life and death are in its hand.
And since, all in one day, there's time
To stretch me on the rack like this,
Why's there not time, all in one day,
To bring me home to happiness?
Is there some natural law says:
Love takes longer than injuries?

Sergeant   You saw her once. You only saw
                      Her an instant. That's foolish, sir.

Captain   No sergeant, it's quite rational.
                      This is my reason: I've seen her.
                      It takes an instant for a spark
                      To set a great forest ablaze.
                      An instant: a volcano roars,
                      Overflows into an abyss.
                      An instant: lightning crashes down,
                      Totally, instantly destroying.
                      An instant: horror flashes from
                      The black mouth of the iron cannon.
                      So why can't love, which after all
                      Flares up in four distinctive ways –
                      Fire, volcano, lightning, cannon –
                      Burn, frighten, wound and devastate?

Sergeant   Didn't you have some theory
                      That peasant girls weren't beautiful?

Captain   That was my firm belief, and that
                      Was the main reason that I fell.
                      When a man enters knowingly
                      A battle area, he goes
                      Expecting to defend himself
                      Against a horde of enemies.
                      But, strolling down a country road,
                      Far from the war, relaxed, that's when
                      He runs the greatest risk of all.
                      The ambush strikes! He's a dead man.
                      I thought I'd find some bumpkin wench –
                      I discovered a fine lady.
                      So obviously I was thrown
                      Off-balance because unready.
                      In my whole life I've never seen
                      A more divine, perfect being.
                      Her face haunts me, Rebolledo,
                      I'd do anything to see it.

Rebolledo   In our squad, sir, there's a fellow
                      Sings like a bloody nightingale,
                      And Chispa, that's my tart, excels
                      At filthy songs and serenades.
                      Post them outside her window, sir,

Tell 'em to hold a party there.
They make a racket. Isabel
Looks out the window. You see her
And maybe chat her up.

Captain   But old
Don Lope sleeps there, that's the snag.
If he wakes up, we're sunk.

Rebolledo   He sleeps
Like the dead with that gammy leg.
Come on, sir. If they rumble us
We'll be the ones to take the rap.
You get a cloak and mandolin
And stand well back, all muffled up
Like a musician with a cold.

Captain   Whether it harms my cause or not
I must do something. Organise
Your friends and meet me here tonight.

[*Exeunt* CAPTAIN *and* SERGEANT]

Chispa   [*Off*]
Take that, you sod!

Rebolledo   Chispa – what's up?

[*Enter* CHISPA *with a dagger*]

Chispa   Nothing. I carved my signature
On some poor bastard's face. He's off.

Rebolledo   Bloody hell. What you do that for?

Chispa   After I've thrown the dice for hours
He tried to diddle me. <u>No tip</u>.
I'd paid up conscientiously
Every time winning spots came up.
He strolled off loaded. Had to teach
Him that a winner tips. He's gone
Down to the barber to get stitched.
Darling, let's get back to our room
So we can settle our accounts.

Rebolledo   A fine thing, to get in a fight
When I feel like some song and dance.

Chispa	The carve-up's over. If you want A party I've got castanets. [CHISPA *produces castanets*] What are we going to sing then?
Rebolledo	No. It's not nocturnal enough yet. We need more instrumentalists, Not just your clackers. So let's find A tavern and get mildly pissed.
Chispa	When I'm dead and really rotten, Let my cut-price gravestone say: Here lies Chispa who was called The mistress of a croupier.

[*Exeunt* REBOLLEDO *and* CHISPA. DON LOPE *and* PEDRO CRESPO *enter the garden or a verandah overlooking the garden.*]

Crespo	The evening air is cooling down. We're both outdoor men, Don Lope. I'll have them bring the table out. We'll dine here more enjoyably. I'll say one thing for August days – They make a good end at nightfall.
Don Lope	Crespo, you've got a garden here I'd call damnably beautiful.
Crespo	It's my daughter's favourite place. She likes to grow flowers and herbs. Sit down and listen: Can you hear? See the breeze's gentle fingers Stroke the tree-tops and the vines And a thousand little leaves purr. At the same time the fountain plays Its silver zither strung with pearls, Striking chords upon the pebbles And the strings of climbing tendrils. Pity our music's limited To instruments, no vocalists, Except the birds, and they insist That they'll not sing once day has passed And I can't force them to. Sit down. The garden will help you forget Your continuous, nagging pain.

[DON LOPE *sits*]

Don Lope	It won't work, Crespo, all the time That damned ache's tugging at my nerves As God's my judge.
Crespo	May He cure you.
Don Lope	At least may He not make it worse. Be seated, Crespo.
Crespo	It's all right.
Don Lope	Be seated.
Crespo	Since you say I may I'll do so gladly sir, although You're not obliged to sit with me.

[CRESPO *sits*]

Don Lope	You're different today, you know? Yesterday, at your anger's height, You weren't yourself at all, were you?
Crespo	I always am myself and I Am nothing else.
Don Lope	Then yesterday Why, when I hadn't said "Sit down" Did you sit down even before I had damn well sat down?
Crespo	Because You had not asked me to sit down. Today, when you did ask me, I Demurred, for I'll show courtesy To anyone who shows it to me.
Don Lope	Just yesterday you yelled about Killing officers and honour. You're a pleasant chap today. Damn it, a gentlemanly man, sir.
Crespo	The reason's this: My principle When spoken to, is to reply In the same way, and the same tone. If you remember, yesterday You spoke to me aggressively So I replied in kind. Besides It's also in my strategy

To swear with swearers and to pray
With those who pray. And in this way,
Through imitation I begin
To understand and sympathise.
So, all last night I lay awake
Attempting to imagine this
Continual pain of yours. By dawn
I had a pain in both my legs.
I had to try both of them for
Which of yours hurts you never said.
So they both ache still. Tell me, please,
Which one gives all the agony –
So I can try to understand
Your burden more accurately?

Don Lope   I've got good reason to complain –
Thirty years in bloody Flanders.
Thirty years of battles fought.
Thirty years of vicious weather –
Frozen in winter, soaked in spring
And in autumn, in the summer baked –
And in those thirty years not one
Hour have I known without this ache.
Imagine all that – if you can.

Crespo   I pray God grant you patience, sir.

Don Lope   My dear sir, I'm not impatient.

Crespo   God keep you so.

Don Lope   Obliged, I'm sure.
But my patience is under siege –
Two thousand demons tear my nerves!
I wish they'd end my misery.

Crespo   They won't. Devils don't do good turns.

Don Lope   Jesus! Ten thousand times! Jesus!

Crespo   May he be with us both, I pray.

Don Lope   I swear to Christ, it's killing me!

Crespo   I swear to Christ, I pity you.

[JUAN *brings out the table for dinner*]

Juan   Where would you like the table, sir?

[CRESPO *shows him*]

Don Lope What? Aren't my servants coming out
To bring our dinner?

Crespo I told them,
If you don't mind, they need not serve
Or buy provisions while you stay
In this house, for, thanks to God,
We are abundantly supplied
With everything that you could need.

Don Lope Since my servants are off-duty
Do me a favour. Please invite
Your daughter here to dine with us.

Crespo [*To* JUAN]
Tell Isabel to come and dine.

[*Exit* JUAN]

Don Lope You understand that my bad health
Places me above suspicion
Where she's concerned, you know?

Crespo Dear sir,
I wish your health were perfect, then
You'd see that I'd never suspect
That you could act dishonourably.
Believe my great respect for you,
For I would trust you utterly.
I told her to remain upstairs
So she wouldn't have to listen
To the usual bantering
And a lot of idle nonsense.
But if soldiers, as a rule,
Had your own courteous ways,
My daughter would most willingly
Serve them at table every day.

Don Lope [*Aside*]
Very cunning for a peasant –
Or he's got a lot of nons.

[*Enter* JUAN, ISABEL *and* INES]

Isabel Sir, what are your orders for me?

Crespo	This gentleman, Don Lope, wants To honour you; he sent for you.
Isabel	I am your humble servant, sir.
Don Lope	Quite the contrary, I'm yours. [*Aside*] There's no doubt, damn it, she's superb. – I should like you to dine with me.
Isabel	Juan and I could wait upon you, Isn't that better?
Don Lope	Please sit down.
Crespo	Obey Don Lope.
Isabel	[*Sitting*] So I do.

[*Guitars and voices heard outside*]

Don Lope	What's that row?
Crespo	Out in the street Some soldiers are fooling around, Singing and dancing.
Don Lope	Well, you see The work of war makes such demands And so does army discipline, That any soldier must relax And when he does, he paints the town.
Juan	It seems a good life for a man.
Don Lope	Would you like to see some action?
Juan	I'd immediately join up If you'd grant me your protection.
Soldier	[*In street*] This looks like a good place to sing.
Rebolledo	Let's have a song for Isabel. That's her window, knock her up then. There's some gravel. Grab a handful.
Crespo	They're serenading somebody. Some girl. [*Aside*] I'll keep my self-control.

Chispa and Soldier

> [*Sing*]
> Little blue flowers of rosemary,
> Isabel, isn't it funny?
> Little blue flowers of rosemary,
> Isabel, isn't it true?
> Little blue flowers of rosemary,
> Tomorrow they'll give me honey.
> Little blue flowers of rosemary,
> Isabel, just like you.

Don Lope

> [*Aside*]
> Music's forgiveable, but stones!
> They're chucking gravel at the place!
> Outside the house where I'm a guest
> They howl their cheapjack serenades.
> Better conceal my anger now
> To save embarrassment to her.
> – Such antics!

Crespo

> Oh, they're only lads.
> [*Aside*] But if Don Lope wasn't here
> I'd give them hell –

Juan

> [*Aside*]
> – If only I
> Could get at that sword which hangs
> In Don Lope's room.

> [JUAN *starts to leave*]

Crespo

> Are you off?

Juan

> Just off to fetch the dinner-things.

Crespo

> We've serving boys to see to that.

All

> [*In street*]
> Isabel! Awaken to me!

Isabel

> What have I ever done to them
> To be abused so shamefully?

Don Lope

> I can't stand it any longer –
> It's disgusting! Damn disgusting!

> [DON LOPE *overturns a chair*]

Crespo

> Yes, I'm with you in your anger.

[CRESPO *overturns a chair*]

Don Lope	I lost my patience. There's a thing. Tell me, isn't it a menace When a leg's so agonizing?
Crespo	That's what made me angry also.
Don Lope	Oh, I thought that you meant something Different when you threw down your chair.
Crespo	Since you overturned your chair, sir, I was obliged to overturn My chair out of courtesy, sir. [*Aside*] My honour – let me see this through.
Don Lope	[*Aside*] If only I were in the street. – Sir, I've decided not to dine. You may retire.
Crespo	Have a good sleep.
Don Lope	God bless you, lady.
Isabel	God bless you.
Don Lope	[*Aside*] Doesn't my window face the street? Haven't I got a sword and shield?
Crespo	[*Aside*] I can sneak out through the yard gate, Taking my old sword on the way.
Don Lope	Good night.
Crespo	[*Aside*] I'll lock my children's doors From the outside.
Don Lope	[*Aside*] I'd better let Everyone settle down.
Isabel	How hopelessly they all pretend Not to be cross.
Ines	[*Aside*] They all pretend To be calm to fool each other.

Crespo	Juan.
Juan	Sir?
Crespo	[*Pointing* JUAN *in opposite direction to the one in which he was going*] Your bedroom.
Juan	Yes, father.

[*Exeunt* ALL *from garden and verandah* . . . CAPTAIN, SERGEANT, CHISPA *and* REBOLLEDO *are in the street with guitars and soldiers.*]

Rebolledo	Move up, lads. Stay out of the light. Let's have more harmony, less talk. I wish I'd brought a tuning-fork.
Chispa	Let's get a ballad going –
Rebolledo	Right.
Chispa	Nothing I'd rather do than sing.
Captain	You could try singing louder but The girl's slammed every shutter shut.
Rebolledo	Don't worry, they're all listening.
Chispa	[*Hearing footsteps*] Wait!
Sergeant	Why? I don't want to get nicked.
Rebolledo	What on earth is it? I can't see.
Chispa	Part of the aristocracy, Heavily armed, but derelict.

[*Enter* DON MENDO *with a shield, and* NUNO]

Don Mendo	Can you see what's afoot?
Nuno	I see Nothing afoot at all, but do Hear something ahead.
Don Mendo	Tell me who Enjoys such caterwauling?
Nuno	Me.
Don Mendo	[*Sings*] Oh Isabel, so pale and frail, Blossom of blossoms, heed my plight.

Hark to your noble nightingale,
Hear in the night your warbling knight.
[*Speaks*]
Do you suppose fair Isabel
Will open her casement?

Nuno   Even so.

Don Mendo   Villain – she will not, will she?

Nuno   No.

Don Mendo   Oh, green-eyed goddess, I'm in hell.
I'll scatter these howling rowdies
With my good blade – No, bold lover!
[*Producing a pretentious penknife*]
Hold your wrath till you discover
Whether this discordant crowd is
Gathered to pillage or to clown.

Nuno   All right then, shall we take a seat?

Don Mendo   A good thought, Nuno. On my feet
I'm more exposed than sitting down.

Rebolledo   Funny, now he's more like a dwarf.
If he's thinking of attacking
This mob, we'll soon send him packing,
A midget ghost, to Lethe's wharf.
Tune up your tonsils, Chispa, we
Want a knock-out song.

Chispa   I've got one.

Rebolledo   Chispa, give us such a hot one
That bloodshed shall ensue –

Chispa   Si, si.

[*Enter* DON LOPE *and* CRESPO *at the same moment, both armed, from opposite sides.*]

Chispa   [*Sings*]
Let me tell you about Sampayo,
He was born with a carver in his hand.
He was a stylish villain when it came to killing
And the best bloody pimp in the land.

Sampayo had a crazy woman,
La Chillona was her name.

In the entire west she was second best
But the number one lay in Spain.

Sampayo went to Garlo's wine shop
For a bottle or two of red –
There was Chillona with the wine shop owner
Drinking brandy in a double bed.

Garlo jumped off of the mattress
And his rapier began to swing
With a forehand slash like a lightning flash
And a backhand like a scorpion sting –

[DON LOPE *and* CRESPO *attack*]

Crespo   Like this?

Don Lope   No – more like this, I think.

[*They chase the soldiers off. Re-enter* DON LOPE]

Extremely brave! All of them flee,
Leaving just one to hold the fort.

[*Re-enter* PEDRO CRESPO]

Crespo   They've run. But at least this one's caught.
I'll teach him country courtesy.

Don Lope   This ruffian is going to pay
With a few pints of blood.

Crespo   I'll beat
This barbarian down our street,
Over the hills and far away.

Don Lope   By heaven, why not run?

Crespo   By hell,
Run if you like, but I won't flee.

Don Lope   By God, he fights efficiently.

Crespo   By God, he handles himself well.

[*Enter* JUAN]

Juan   I hope my father's winning this.
– I'm at your side, sir. Let me fight.

Don Lope   Is that you, Crespo?

Crespo   Yes, that's right.
Is that Don Lope?

Don Lope	Yes it is. Didn't you promise me that you Wouldn't come out tonight? So – why?
Crespo	Let my excuse and my reply Be that I did what you did too.
Don Lope	This brawl was an insult to me, Not you.
Crespo	Well, I must not pretend . . . I came out because you did, friend, To fight in your good company.
Soldier	[*Off*] Come on you bastards, let's get back And massacre the whole damn town.

[*Enter* CAPTAIN, SERGEANT, REBOLLEDO, CHISPA *and* SOLDIERS]

Captain	Christ, that's enough now. Keep it down.
Don Lope	Captain, are you a maniac?
Captain	The men, sir, got into a brawl They were proceeding to their mess Singing, but without rowdiness And we've had no complaints at all. Then somehow they got in a fight Which I then did my best to quell.
Don Lope	I understand you very well Don Alvaro, and since tonight This area seems to attract Trouble, it's my will and pleasure To lay down a simple measure Which you'll immediately enact. I command, upon the grounds Of this dubious affray: March out your soldiers. From today, Zalamea's out of bounds. Should such a rumpus reoccur I shall visit a horrendous Punishment on the offenders, By God, with my own rapier.
Captain	Certainly sir. That's what we'll do. Today the company shall go.

[*Aside*] Beautiful Isabel. I know
I'm going to lose my life for you.

Crespo

[*Aside*]
We get on well now, there's no doubt,
Despite his eccentricity.

Don Lope

Come on, Crespo, I shall see
Nobody pushes you about.

[*Exeunt*]

◇

[*A forest outside Zalamea. Day. Enter* DON MENDO *and*
NUNO.]

Don Mendo

Are you wounded seriously,
Nuno?

Nuno

Well, I'm pretty sure
I'm not wounded humourously.
This will suffice, I need no more.

Don Mendo

Never in all my history
Has my heart felt so desolate.

Nuno

Nor mine.

Don Mendo

I feel my anger ride
Righteously. Did that reprobate
Strike my own servant on the pate?

Nuno

No. On the nose, chin, ears and eyes.

[*A bugle sounds*]

Don Mendo

What's that?

Nuno

The soldiers march away.

Don Mendo

Why then, today's my lucky day.
To jealousy I say farewell –
The Captain can't woo Isabel.

Nuno

They march before nightfall, they say.

[*Enter* CAPTAIN *and* SERGEANT]

Captain	Sergeant, keep marching with your men Until the night arrives, and when The great sun goes to his dark home In the Atlantic's freezing foam I'll be waiting among these Overshadowing forest trees. Tonight I'll make my life arise To fly high with an eagle's ease – I shall be born as the sun dies.
Sergeant	Look out, sir, someone passing by – One of the local madmen.
Don Mendo	[*To* NUNO] <div align="center">Try</div>To slip past them. Better act tough If we're seen.
Nuno	<div align="right">Act tough? It's enough</div>To make a money-lender cry.
	[*Exeunt* DON MENDO *and* NUNO]
Captain	Whatever happens, I must go Back to plead with my love again. I've bribed her serving-maid and so I may see Isabel although She murders me with her disdain. It took some trinkets to persuade Her servant she must be betrayed.
Sergeant	Sir, if you're dead set to make a Second visit, better take a Bodyguard, or a brigade. Those peasants will be guarding her.
Captain	You're quite right, Sergeant. Have you got Enough men I can trust?
Sergeant	<div align="right">Yes, sir.</div>We've got some good blokes in our lot – No problems there at all. But sir, What if Don Lope catches you?
Captain	Most fortunately he's been sent To Guadalupe to review And to prepare the regiment. The King gets there any moment.

Sergeant	I'll go and pick the lads to take.
Captain	And brief them well. My life's at stake.

[*Exit* SERGEANT. *Enter* REBOLLEDO *and* CHISPA]

Rebolledo	You've something to be grateful for To me, sir.
Captain	Grateful? Tell me more.
Rebolledo	You know that lad? Old Crespo's son? He's joined the army. So you've one Enemy less. He's off to war. You see, Don Lope asked his Dad If he could spare the little lad, And Crespo. as you might well guess, Spluttered a bit, and then said yes. Isabel's brother's gone – how sad! I saw him just now in the square, Shaved for the first time, all spruced up, A brand-new soldier with the air Of an ex-peasant – like a pup Crossed with a cat – I had to stare . . . Which all boils down to this – we can Be sure there's only the old man To guard the girl.
Captain	That's marvellous. And I've bribed a maid to help us To execute my little plan. Suddenly things are going well. Tonight, perhaps, I'll be with Isabel.
Rebolledo	You can bet on it, sir.
Captain	You two, You'll come with me. I've work to do. Meet you soon, and then – who can tell?

[*Exit* CAPTAIN]

Rebolledo	By Christ, there'd be too few of us Even if we had, say, ten more, Or twenty-two. Or eighty-four.
Chispa	And what about me? I don't fuss But I've been left behind before. Advise me. What am I to do

If I'm battered by that robber
I carved up?

Rebolledo   What could we do with you?
You wouldn't have the guts to join our crew.

Chispa   Guts? Yes. I simply haven't got the clobber.

Rebolledo   A uniform? Well, I can lift
The costume off some page-boy. It's a gift.

Chispa   Some adjustments and I might
Pass for a boy in dimmish light.

Rebolledo   A boy. I've not seen nothing yet.

[*Trumpets sound*]

Chispa   Oh, now I understand
My dear old mother's song:

[*Sings*] "A soldier's love is less
Than twenty minutes long."

[*Exeunt* REBOLLEDO *and* CHISPA]

◇

[*Pedro Crespo's house. Enter* DON LOPE, PEDRO CRESPO *and* JUAN]

Don Lope   I'm grateful for so many things
You've given me as a friend and host
But above all for your young son
Whom you've permitted to enlist.
By my soul, damn it, I'm quite moved.
I guess how much it costs your heart.

Crespo   He'll be your servant always, sir.

Don Lope   I take him as comrade-in-arms.
I've been impressed most favourably
By his coolness and fortitude
And his eagerness in a fight.

Juan   I dedicate my life to you
And my death too. You'll understand
This from the total way in which I serve
With absolute obedience.

Crespo	One request I'd mention, dear sir:
	Please pardon him if he commits
	Errors in service etiquette,
	For in this university –
	The country – he's a graduate
	In ploughshare, thresher, spade, hoe, rake,
	Wheelbarrow, harness and pitchfork.
	He's never seen a palace or
	Mixed with sophisticated folk,
	So if he's ever impolite
	Please put it down to ignorance.
Don Lope	Don't worry. But it's getting dark.
	Sir, we shall have to leave at once.
Juan	Your litter-bearers should be here.
	I'll fetch them sir.

[*Exit* JUAN. *Enter* ISABEL *and* INES]

Isabel	Is this polite –
	To leave without saying farewell
	To one who'd serve you all her life?
Don Lope	I'd not have left until I had
	Kissed both your hands and asked you this:
	Will you excuse my shamelessness
	In offering this worthless gift?
	The thought behind it, that's the thing.
	This part has a few diamonds,
	Not bad ones, but they seem too dim
	Now that I place it in your hands.
	But please take this medallion,
	Accept it, wear it in my name.
Isabel	I'm very touched. But we owe you
	A gift for honouring our home.
	You owe us nothing sir, except
	Your promise to return again.
Don Lope	This does not represent a debt
	But affection. Just a token.
Isabel	I accept it as affection
	And not as payment. Now I put
	My brother Juan into your care
	Knowing he is most fortunate
	To be allowed to serve you, sir.

Don Lope	I can assure you that your young Hot-headed brother will do well. I've taken him under my wing.

[Enter JUAN]

Juan	Your litter's ready for you, sir.
Don Lope	God bless you.
Crespo	May this God of ours Protect you, sir.
Don Lope	Oh Crespo, you're A good man.
Crespo	Oh, Don Lope, you're Invincible.
Don Lope	Who would have said When we met after that bother Up in the attic, that we'd change Into a couple of blood-brothers?
Crespo	I would have said, sir, there and then, From how you acted, that I thought You were a . . .
Don Lope	Tell me, damn it, man.
Crespo	. . . A crackpot with a mighty heart.

[Exit DON LOPE]

Crespo	While Don Lope gets comfortably Settled into his litter, Juan, I've some advice, to be witnessed By your sister and your cousin. Son, by the grace of God, you come From a most honourable line. Your name's untarnished as the sun And – you're a peasant in your bones. Why do I tell you these two things? One, so you won't make the mistake Of undervaluing yourself But keep your pride and always work To build yourself a better life. Two, so that you won't over-reach, Pretending to be what you're not

And so demeaning what you are.
Equally, when you're in pursuit
Of both these aims, go humbly for
Thus you'll find out what's wrong, what's right,
And, knowing this, you can ignore
Whatever bad example's set
By haughty, so-called gentlemen.
We've all met people who are known
To be imperfect in some way
And yet the world excuses them
Because of their humility.
Likewise there are others who are
Honest and affable, but they
Are generally disliked because
They're lacking in humility.
Be courteous to everyone
And when you can, be generous.
For kind words and an open house
Help to attract good friends to us.
All of the gold in Mexico
That grows engendered by the sun,
All sunken treasure – it's worthless
Beside the good name of a man.
A word on women: never speak
Maliciously of them. The worst
Of them deserves a man's respect
Because a woman gave him birth.
Don't get in fights without good cause . . .
Sometimes in town I see a sign
Proclaiming some swordmaster who
Says "Let me teach you how to fight".
I think that's wrong, for I believe
We shouldn't teach young men the skill
Of slaughtering each other but
Why and when it is right to kill.
I'm sure one fencing master who
Hung up a sign which said, boldly:
"I'll teach you when to fight", would find
He had a packed academy.
With this advice, accept these coins,
Partly to spend along the way,
Partly so, on your arrival,
You can have two uniforms made.
Don Lope will protect you and

> You have my blessing. And my prayers.
> May we meet soon. Goodbye my son.
> I'm too moved to say any more.

Juan
> I will remember your advice
> It has been carefully engraved
> Upon my heart and, while I live,
> There these good wise words will remain.
> Now give me your hand, sir, and you
> Sister, embrace me quickly, for
> Don Lope, my lord, is leaving.

Isabel
> My arms would gladly keep you here.

Juan
> Cousin Ines, goodbye.

Ines
>   I can't
> Say farewell properly, my eyes
> Are choking me with silly tears
> So I only say – goodbye.

Crespo
> Go well and go quickly my son
> For a prolonged goodbye like this
> Tempts me to beg you not to go.
> But you must, for I have promised.

Juan
> May God remain here with you all.

> [*Exit* JUAN]

Crespo
> May God travel along with you.

Isabel
> Sending him off is cruelty.

Crespo
> If I turn, and don't watch him go,
> I can speak more soberly.
> At home, how'd he have spent his time?
> His days in taverns or in bed,
> His nights in love or gambling games –
> Much better go and serve his King.

Isabel
> I'm worried that he leaves at night.

Crespo
> Travelling is far worse by day.
> On the march in summertime
> Is hellish work, horses and men
> Sizzle and fry in their own sweat.
> He'll soon catch up with Don Lope.
> [*Aside*] I must put a brave face on it.

Isabel
> Come sir, shall we go indoors now?

Ines	Now there are no soldiers left, Let's stay out a little longer So we can enjoy the fresh Breath of the breeze. And soon we'll see Friends on their evening promenade.
Crespo	Well, as for me, I'll stay outside. From here I almost see the road And I imagine how its dust Gleams whitely underneath the tread Of my son's horse. I almost see Juan as he rides, so young and proud. Ines, I'd like to sit down here Beside the doorway.
Ines	Here's a stool.
Isabel	The town council elected their New officers this afternoon.
Crespo	Yes, well it's August, that's the month They hold elections in.

[CRESPO *sits. Enter* CAPTAIN, SERGEANT, REBOLLEDO, CHISPA *as a page, and* SOLDIERS.]

Captain	No noise. Rebolledo – inform that maid That I'm outside her master's house. She knows what to do next.
Rebolledo	I'm off. – But sir, there's people over there.
Sergeant	Yes. Look how the moonbeams catch One person in particular. That looks like Isabel.
Captain	It is. I would have known without the moon – My heart told me immediately. We've come at the right moment, men. If, now that we've gone this far, We hazard everything, this won't Have been a wasted journey.
Sergeant	Sir, Do you want my advice?
Captain	I don't.

Sergeant	Right sir, that's fair enough, I'll keep Mum and try not to reason why.
Captain	I shall walk over to that door And carry Isabel away. At the same time, you draw your swords. Stop anyone following me.
Sergeant	Right sir, we've come this far with you We'll fit in with your strategy.
Captain	Listen to me everybody We rendezvous back in that wood Beside that big rock on the right Just before the two roads divide.
Rebolledo	Chispa?
Chispa	Yes.
Rebolledo	Hold these cloaks.
Chispa	All right. The joy of fighting I suppose Is like the joy of swimming, it's Spoiled if some bastard steals your clothes.
Captain	I must be first to tackle them.
Crespo	The best part of the evening's gone. Let's go inside.
Captain	It must be now. Now! Are you ready! Friends, come on!
Isabel	Sir! The Captain? What's this, sir?
Captain	Delirium maybe. Madness. Love.

[CAPTAIN *carries* ISABEL *off and exits, while his companions restrain* CRESPO *with their swords.*]

Isabel	[*Off*] You traitor.
Crespo	Oh you cowards.
Isabel	[*Off*] Help!
Crespo	Ines, inside [INES *runs into the house*] So you perceive That I've no sword, you godless scum You treacherous, poisonous lice.

Rebolledo	Piss off old man, unless you want To be cut up like Flemish lace.

[*Exit* REBOLLEDO *and servants*]

Crespo	You've killed my honour, why, by God Should I be keen to stay alive? Christ, where's my sword? If I go now And follow them unarmed, the cause Is hopeless. But if I decide To fetch a sword, when I return They'll have vanished. Which do I choose? I've got two choices – either one Leads to the same black hopelessness.

[*Enter* INES *with his sword*]

Ines	[*Giving him his sword*] I've brought your sword, sir.

[*Exit* INES]

Crespo	In good time. And now my honour has come back to me. I was helpless as a baby, But now – God help my enemies.

[*Exit* CRESPO]

◇

[*The forest outside Zalamea.* CRESPO *fighting against* REBOLLEDO, SERGEANT, CHISPA *and* SOLDIERS]

Crespo	Let go of me, you renegades. I'll get the girl back, or fighting Die, but before you cut me down I'll scratch you devils –
Sergeant	– Pack it in, It's five to one, and that's poor odds.
Crespo	How many wounds? I've lost count. Why, The whole pack's fighting against me. [CRESPO *falls*] I didn't fall. The ground gave way.
Rebolledo	Finish him off.

Sergeant	You vicious sod, We took his daughter didn't we? And his precious honour too? Enough's enough. No cruelty. I've got some rope. We'll tie him up, Leave him in the wood, well-hidden So he can't go and mobilise A mob of enraged citizens.
Isabel	[*Off*] Father!
Crespo	Isabel!
Rebolledo	Take him off And truss him up the way you said.
Crespo	Isabel! They won't let me go.

[*Exit all* SOLDIERS *with* CRESPO]

Isabel	[*Off*] Father!

[*Enter* JUAN]

Juan	As I was riding past this wood My horse fell and then bolted off At top speed and I have followed, Blindly charging through the brambles. And then I heard a young girl's cry. And then I heard an old man's groan. Another scream. Another sigh. Not clear, but muffled. And so I Face two necessities. Both need My championship, and both of them Cry out with equal urgency. One's an old man, and one's a girl. I'll save the lady if I can And thus show my obedience To my father's two commands. "Honour all women", he told me. "Fight for good reasons only." Right. I'll go to defend this woman And, with a perfect motive, fight.

[*Exit* JUAN]

[*End of Act Two*]

Act Three

[*The forest.* ISABEL *is alone, weeping*]

Isabel

I never want to see the light,
The lovely light, ever again,
I never want to see myself,
My shameful self, ever again.
Night sky, with your dark blue meadows
Bright with a million star-flowers,
Don't let the dawn walk towards me
With that young sunshine smile of hers.
If you can't keep the dawn away,
Let her come with eyes full of rain,
Not mocking me with laughing light.

King of all planets, mighty Sun,
Just for this once, wait down below
The cold sea a little longer.
Just for this once, let the shy night
Rule her shining, trembling empire
A little longer, hiding me.
Sun-God, let it be said of you:
He listened to her graciously
And, because he decided to
He granted everything she asked.
Why do you want to rise at all
To read my story – this cruel,
Cold-blooded act, a tale as vile
As has been told about the way
Men revenge themselves on women?

No? You're a tyrant. Even as I
Beg you to delay arriving
A little longer, here you come,
Striding along, face towering
Over the trees' tall green shadows.
I've angered you. You've been plotting.
You're part of the conspiracy
To cut my honour into shreds.
What can I do? Where can I go?
If I go home, my father's wide
Wound will gape wider, horribly.

How he loved to see his honour.
Reflected in the moon of mine.
Moon . . . a bad sun has eclipsed her,
My honour's blotted out. No light.
And if I don't go home, from fear
And from respect for him – they'll say
I encouraged my attacker
And call me hypocritical.

My brother came by here just now.
I ran away. I should've stayed.
I should have stayed and let him know
What happened to me. And I should
Have let him, in his righteous rage,
Kill me. I'll shout to him. He'll come
And kill me, kill me right away.
I'll scream out what's been done to me
Until it echoes –

Crespo   [*Off*]
                              Come back. Kill me.
Murderer, please be merciful
And kill me, for there's no mercy
In leaving such a wretch alive.

Isabel   Whose is that voice, broken and frail
So I can hardly hear its words?

Crespo   [*Off*]
Kill me, if you'd be merciful.

                    [ISABEL *finds* CRESPO *tied up*]

Crespo   If anyone who walks this wood
Wishes to help a wretched soul –

Isabel   It's him. My father and my lord.

Crespo   My daughter. Come here, Isabel,
Come and untie these ropes.

Isabel   My lord
I daren't. If I untied you now
I'd never dare to tell to you
The story of my grief and how
I've been maltreated. You'd kill me
Before I'd properly explained,
Because your honour's gone. But please
First let me tell you all my pain.

Crespo	Isabel, please understand this. There are some stories, Isabel, Which don't need a story-teller.
Isabel	What has happened, and what I feel, You have to know, I have to tell. And even while you're listening You'll be enraged and want revenge Before you take in everything. Only yesterday evening I can remember how we both Enjoyed peace and security – Your grey age guarding my green youth. But then, deciding honour's made To be outfoxed by villainy, Those traitors, muffled in their cloaks, Crept up to us, stole me away, Just as a lean, bloodthirsty wolf Snatches an innocent young lamb Out of the flock.

And that Captain,
That guest who, on the day he came,
Showed his ingratitude to you
With that amazing disturbance,
With treacherous and cunning tricks,
With bad feeling and arguments –
He was the one who snatched me up.
Meanwhile his fellow-Judases
Covered his cowardly retreat.
This forest was his hiding place.
In all ages such tangled, dark
Forests are chosen by the strong
When they choose to torment the weak.

And here I found myself, alone,
Alone with him. During the chase
I'd heard you calling to me but
The wind arose, and by degrees
Your words were scattered in the air
Fainter and fainter, till your voice
Turned to an echo, which became
An echo's memory; just as
After you've heard a trumpet call
It's still there when it's stopped sounding,
Not as a real sound of course

But an impression, lingering.
Then your voice vanished. And he knew
Now nobody was following
And nobody could save me now.
Even the moon was not looking,
She hid under a cloak of clouds,
That cold, revengeful little moon,
Hoarding away each particle
Of light she borrows from the sun.

Despite my terrible distress
The traitor tried, with urgent lies
To find excuses for his love,
The kind of love that tries to force
Unwanted kisses on someone
Who's utterly repelled by them.
I lay my curse upon the man,
I lay my deepest curse on him
Who tries, by force, to steal a heart.
He is cursed, for he doesn't see
That victory in love, the prize,
Consists in winning peacefully
The beauty which he so admires . . .
Men can make love by force, of course,
And boast they've loved a beauty, but
They've only made love to a corpse.

Well, so I pleaded with the man,
Firmly said I could not love him,
Spoke to him humbly, with disdain,
Angrily, but nothing moved him.
Then (let my voice fall silent now)
His arrogance (my throat was tight)
His boldness(my heart screamed aloud)
His rudeness (my eyes cried and cried)
His fierceness (yelling in my ears)
His cruelty (I could not breathe)
His shamelessness (for now I'll wear
Mourning until my longed-for death) . . .

There are things my voice cannot say.
Perhaps I can <u>show</u> what I mean.
My tears show my embarrassment.
I hide my face to show my shame.
I clasp my hands to show my grief.

My bosom heaves to show my rage.
I have no words to tell this thing.
You must interpret this display.

And so . . . as the winds repeated my
Desperate, weary moans and sighs
In which I'd first asked God for help
But now cried out for his justice . . .
Dawn came to light the forest paths.
I heard twigs cracking underfoot.
I peered through misty air to see
Who came – and there my brother stood.
In pale half-light he understood
What outrage had been committed,
For grief is quick to comprehend
Catastrophe, grief's sharp-sighted.
Juan did not speak, but drew the sword
You yourself gave him yesterday.
The Captain, being challenged now,
Advanced, drawing his own white blade.
They closed, they clashed, sword against sword,
Thrust and parry, hard they fought,
But while he fought, Juan could not know
If I had been to blame or not.
So that I shouldn't lose my life
Before the truth could be explained,
I turned and through the intertwined
Branches and thorns I ran away
And found a place where branches formed
A screen of leaves. And there I hid
To watch, because escape was less
To me than how the fight ended.
The fight: swiftly my brother's sword
Slashes the Captain, who steps back
And falls. Now Juan is about
To kill him off, when, at his back,
Appear the Captain's men shouting:
Revenge! Revenge! Juan wants to fight
But he's outnumbered hopelessly
And so he beats a quick retreat.

The soldiers argue, but decide
Not to pursue my brother, for
Revenge is less important now
They have a wounded officer.

They bear the Captain in their arms
Back on the road towards the town
Less worried that he'll be arraigned
Than that he's dying of his wound.

I was torn with anxieties.
My mind full of a thousand fears,
Each fear chained to another fear.
I could not breathe, or see, or hear.
I wandered. I fell down. I ran
Without a guiding star or light,
All through the forest till I fell
And lie, exhausted at your feet.

Now that I've told you everything,
I'm ready for your sword. Be brave.
My hands will soon have you untied
And then my life is yours to take.
This rope would do to strangle me.
It is true I am your daughter.
It is true I have no honour.
You are free to kill me, father.
Do it, when I'm dead they'll say:
That man, to give life to his honour,
Did what he had to do and gave
Death, a good gift, to his daughter.

Crespo   Stand up, Isabel, stand up now.
You mustn't stay upon your knees.
No. Without all these cruelties,
Goodness would not be so precious.
We're meant to endure sufferings,
To bear them with courageous hearts.
Isabel, now we must go home,
The boy's in danger. We'll move fast,
Find him and then ensure he's safe.

Isabel   At last. Whatever happens now
My father will watch over me.
He will do everything he can.

Crespo   We'll go.
I'm certain that the Captain's been
Forced to go back into the town
Seeking a doctor for his wound.
And if he dies in utmost pain,

He will have earned it, and will be
Thankful he's spared the thousand pains
I'd kill him with so ardently.
Come now, my daughter, let's go home.

[*Exit* CRESPO *and* ISABEL]

◇

[*The street in front of Pedro Crespo's house*]

[*Enter* PEDRO CRESPO *and* ISABEL. *Enter, meeting them, a* CLERK]

Clerk   Pedro Crespo! Thank me now, sir!

Crespo   What on earth should I thank you for?

Clerk   The town council's chosen you, sir,
To be mayor and magistrate.
Your first day in authority
And two significant events!
First, the King will arrive today
Or in the morning, we expect.
Second: some soldiers have been seen
Secretly bearing into town
For treatment and recovery
That Captain who, just yesterday,
Was here with his whole company.
He's wounded, but how, they won't say.
It's an exciting case, and when
The man's tried – you're the magistrate.

Crespo   [*Aside*]
God in Heaven! My honour was
Ready to take revenge and now
The rod of justice is upraised
To beat my angry honour down.
To kill even that Captain is
Clearly against the law, so how
Can I do that when I've been made
Guardian of justice in this town?
A curious decision this
And I need time to work it out.
[*To* CLERK]
You honour me most highly, sir.
Accept my thanks with all my heart.

Clerk	Shall we go to the Town Hall, sir? First the councillors will acclaim You as their Mayor, then you'll call Witnesses about this Captain.
Crespo	We shall go. Isabel, you Go into our house and stay there.
Isabel	Let me come.
Crespo	Justice will be done For you, your father's now the mayor.

[ISABEL *exits into the house,* CRESPO *and* CLERK *down the street.*]

◇

[*The Captain's lodgings. The* CAPTAIN, *with his wound bandaged, and the* SERGEANT]

Captain	A scratch – as if my skin had caught Upon a thorn, he said. That's great. Why bring me back here?
Sergeant	Had to wait Till we knew what the doctor thought.
Captain	Now it's been seen, cleaned and bound Don't you reckon we should make A run for it, for my health's sake Before it's known that I'm around?
Sergeant	It was a risk we had to take. You were all bloody. Bloody hell.
Captain	Seeing I'm now alive and well, Staying in town's a bad mistake. Before they're guarding every street We'd better shift. Collect my gear. Where have the others gone?
Sergeant	They're here.
Captain	Good. We must beat a swift retreat From these peasants. They're poisonous. And when they hear that girl's story And find out I'm still here, they'll be Delighted to massacre us.

[*Enter* REBOLLEDO]

Rebolledo   Excuse me, sir, the law's outside.

Captain   What's civil law to do with me?

Rebolledo   I don't know, sir, I thought you'd be
Interested. Sorry. If I'd –

Captain   The law's here. Let it do its job.
Now everybody knows we're here,
Civilian law's nothing to fear
Compared with a clodhopping mob
Who'd most gladly crucify us.
Arrested soldiers, legally,
Must go to the military –
Only such a court can try us.
I may lose rank and pay and more
But my life's safe.

Rebolledo   They say the court
Heard the girl's story.

Captain   So I thought.

Crespo   [*Off*]
Guard every window! Every door!
None of the soldiers who've been seen
Scuttling into this house today
Must be allowed to get away –
Shoot all who try –

Captain   What does this mean –
Breaking and entering? [*Aside*] What's this?

[*Enter* PEDRO CRESPO *with rod of office and robes, with armed*
FARMERS]

Crespo   Justice must enter everywhere,
And I'm her servant. So I dare
Go anywhere.

Captain   Such a justice
Must be the cheapest whore in town
If she takes your form overnight.
Look in the mirror – what a sight!
Get out, sir!

Crespo   Keep your temper down.
Let's talk together civilly.
I come officially, indeed,

But not to harm you, and you need
Do nothing but converse with me,
Alone if possible –

Captain   [*To* SERGEANT *and* REBOLLEDO]
Get out.

Crespo   [*To* FARMERS]
Gentlemen, will you leave me here?
[*To* CLERK]
Guard those two soldiers, or I fear
They'll make a run for it.

Clerk   No doubt.

[*Exeunt* FARMERS, CLERK *and* SOLDIERS]

Crespo   I just used my official robes
And rod of office to persuade
You to respect my new-found rank
And listen. Now I set aside
These, for I wish to speak to you
About my troubles, man to man,
[CRESPO *lays aside robes and rod*]
Not the Mayor to the Captain.
And now we're face to face, alone.
So, Don Alvaro, let's both talk
Openly, showing all we feel,
Each emotion now locked up
In our breasts' deep prison cells.
Let's allow them to break out
From those deep, vile, silent dungeons.
Captain, I'm an honest man.
I don't boast of my origins
But, God's truth, wouldn't change my state
From peasant to aristocrat.
If titles were my heart's desire
I could afford to buy a crate.
I live among my equals here
And they've always respected me.
The council too has honoured me
And the municipality.
My lands are very wide, well-run
And richer than you could imagine.
In short sir, there is no farmer
Wealthier in all this region.

My daughter, sir. She's been brought up
With her late mother's character:
Unselfish, highly virtuous,
Well-spoken of, always sheltered
From poverty and viciousness.
To prove to you her goodness – well
I think that it's enough to say:
Although I'm rich, there's no one who'll
Gossip of me or Isabel –
This, understand, in a small town
Where our sole prevailing fault is
To mull over, not our own
But others' lives and shortcomings
And, God above! We always fail
To agree who's most in the wrong.

My daughter's very beautiful.
Well, you're aware of that or you
Would not have acted as you did.
I wish I didn't have to speak . . .
I'd weep – and leave the rest unsaid.
Her beauty's my misfortune, sir.
I'll stop, before we swallow down
All of the poison from that cup.
To test our strength – let some remain.
What's happened must not be allowed
To overwhelm us totally.
What's happened must be made to look
Less like a great monstrosity.
What's happened is so mountainous
It can't be covered up at all
Or God knows I would bury it
In the grave of my mourning soul.
And then I would not come to you
Or argue like this, for you see
What's happened would then only be
A secret tearing inside me.

The sickness is so evident –
Some cure must be open to me.
To kill you? Honour remains sick –
That's revenge, not a remedy.
I've looked at it from every side
And I can only see one way
I'd accept and you might accept,

This: you take all my property –
My house, my money and my land.
Neither my son nor I will keep
A penny, we'll be beggarmen.
And, if you wish, brand both of us
With red-hot irons, and in chains
Stand us upon the auction block
And sell us for obedient slaves,
And thus you'll raise a further sum
Beyond the dowry of your bride.
Give me my reputation back.
I believe you won't be dishonoured.
Sir, you'll have sons, and all the shame
Of being grandchildren of mine
Will be erased, for they will live
As sons of yours, as noblemen.
As the Castilian proverb says:
"The stallion makes up for the mare."
[*Kneels*]
Look, on my knees I beg you now,
By these tears and these grey hairs.
What am I begging for? I beg
For honour. Give it back to me.
Although it's mine, it seems to be
Something of yours, because I plead
For it with such humility.
You know that I am empowered
To take. But I want you to give.

Captain   Old man, my patience has expired.
Of all the blabber-mouthed old bores!
Think yourself lucky that I'm not
A shit – I'd kill you on the spot
Along with that damn son of yours.
I only spare you for the sake
Of pretty little Isabel.
She's really beautiful. Ah well.
Now look, if you intend to take
Revenge on me, see if you can,
Pick up a sword, I'll trust to fate.
[CAPTAIN *waits,* CRESPO *doesn't move*]
Then try me, mister magistrate.
You can't – for I'm an army man.

Crespo   Sir, aren't you moved to see me weep?

Captain	I never cry myself, but when Women, children and old men Cry, I always think: tears are cheap.
Crespo	Can't you console me in some way?
Captain	This consolation I will give: Indulgently, I'll let you live.
Crespo	Look, I prostrate myself! I pray: My good name. Give it back to me.
Captain	You bore me.
Crespo	In Zalamea I am magistrate and mayor.
Captain	You don't listen. Judicially I have to have a court-martial. Civil courts aren't so impartial. The tribunal will send for me, And officers will do the judging. Fined a month's wages, maybe less . . .
Crespo	You're quite determined not to –
Captain	– Yes.
Crespo	[*Standing, donning robes and taking rod of office*] I swear to God That for all this – you'll pay me back. Come in!
	[*Enter the* FARMERS, *armed*]
Clerk	[*Off*] Sir!
Captain	[*Aside*] What are these peasants Going to do?
Farmer	Your orders, sir?
Crespo	You will arrest this officer And remove him from my presence.
Captain	You've gone too far now! Legally I am a servant of the King And it's impossible to fling Me into gaol.

Crespo	Let's try and see. You leave arrested or deceased.
Captain	I warn you Crespo, one more time. I'm a soldier, this is wartime.
Crespo	I'm the mayor, I know no peace. Surrender now. Go to your cell.
Captain	I can't defend myself, so I Have no choice but to comply But I promise you I'll tell The King of this unjust assault.
Crespo	And I shall let our great King know Of an unjust assault also And let him judge who's most at fault. It won't be long now, he's nearby . . . It's best if, of your own accord, You surrender now. Sir – your sword.
Captain	I don't see any reason why.
Crespo	It's customary, I think you'll find.
Captain	Better show some respect for me.
Crespo	Let me assure you, Captain, we Will bear that very much in mind. [*To* FARMERS] Respectfully, stick him in gaol. Fetter his arms and legs and neck To the wall, but with respect. Give him bread, water and a pail Respectfully. And watch him well, But with respect, so he can't plot With his gang. And throw that lot Each in a separate cell And with respect fetter them too. And later, most respectfully, Visit them individually So that they may confess to you. [*To the* CAPTAIN] Captain, in confidence, what you Must do is simply wait and see. And if, by God, you're found guilty, With respect, I shall garrotte you.

Captain   Peasants in power – what an age!

                   [CAPTAIN *is taken out under arrest. Enter the* CLERK, REBOLLEDO *and*
                   CHISPA]

Clerk   One soldier made his getaway
                   But, after an intense affray,
                   We grabbed this person and his page.

Crespo   This one sings. Recall the time
                   You caterwauled to me? Well, soon
                   A noose will help you change your tune.

Rebolledo   Since when has singing been a crime?

Crespo   I think it's wonderful to sing.
                   And so I keep an instrument
                   To whose precise accompaniment
                   You'll warble about everything.
                   Your concert must be good. Rehearse.

Rebolledo   What shall I sing of?

Crespo   Last night –

Rebolledo   Why
                   Your daughter knows better than I
                   What happened.

Crespo   Sing or die or worse.

Chispa   Rebolledo, you must be strong.
                   Deny each charge, admit no point,
                   And, though they tear you joint from joint,
                   You'll be hero of a song
                   I shall compose –

Crespo   You will sing next
                   On my programme.

Chispa   But I can't be
                   Tortured, I've got immunity.

Crespo   Can you quote me your legal text?

Chispa   Under the clause Acquit-me-quick
                   Exculpation must override
                   When accused has good cause inside –

Crespo   What do you mean?

Chispa	I'm up the stick.
Crespo	What is this uniform for, then?
Chispa	To hide my shame. It's all I had.
Crespo	It's clear that you're no serving-lad.
Chispa	Right, sir. I only serve grown men.

Crespo   Enough of this. Best save your breath
            To make your statements.

Chispa   Yes, quite so.
            We'll tell you everything we know
            And more. We're not allured by death.

Crespo   If you confess every detail
            There'll be no torture.

Chispa   Then we will.
            God knows that I was born to trill –
            I'll chirrup like a nightingale:
            [Sings]
            They've got me down for torturing.

Rebolledo   [Sings]
            What do they want to do with me?

Crespo   What's this?

Chispa   Practising harmony.
            We're going to sing, sing, sing, sing!

[REBOLLEDO and CHISPA are led out]

◇

[A room in Crespo's house. Enter JUAN]

Juan   After the fight, after the chase
            By my outnumbering enemies,
            I searched among the forest trees
            For Isabel – but not a trace.
            Finally I've come home to face
            My father, knowing he is wise
            And can probably devise
            A way of healing our disgrace.

[Enter ISABEL and INES]

Ines	What use is mourning? It's too late. To view the world so salty-eyed Is not living, but suicide.
Isabel	Don't you know that it's life I hate?
Juan	There's Isabel. Poor girl. I will Take some action before she sees What I intend to do –

[JUAN *pulls out a dagger*]

Isabel	Brother, please, What are you going to do?
Juan	To kill. You risked my life and my good name And I must be revenged –
Ines	You fool!
Isabel	No. Listen.
Juan	As the heavens rule The earth, I'll kill you –

[*Enter* CRESPO *and the* FARMERS]

Crespo	Who's to blame For this?
Juan	My honour is at stake. I have been done an injury And she must pay the penalty.
Crespo	Enough, enough. It's a mistake For you to stand in front of me – Daring to talk of your honour, For now I represent the law And it's alleged you wantonly Wounded a servant of the King.
Juan	If I committed this offence I was conducting the defence Of your own honour, and fighting –
Crespo	Here, take this one away as well – Arrest him!
Juan	Should your own son be Treated with such severity?

Crespo	I'd put my father in a cell And have him treated just the same. [*Aside*] This ensures he's not attacked And appears such a selfless act Crespo's justice gets a good name.
Juan	Let me explain before I go. After escaping with my life I saw my sister, drew my knife Because I –
Crespo	– I already know, But only as your father. See, I must be told as magistrate. There'll be a trial. Truth must wait To be found out judicially. I'm a mere mayor, not a prophet So I can't know if this grave charge Will have you hanged or set at large. [*Aside*] I'll find some way to get him off it.
Juan	Well, I won't try to prophesy How you'll end up. Your honour's hurt By <u>her</u>, yet you drag <u>me</u> in the dirt And grant her your protection. Why?

[JUAN *is taken away under arrest*]

Crespo	Isabel, please come to my side. Sign this complaint, if it's all true, About the man who outraged you.
Isabel	But it was you who wished to hide Our family's foul injury, And now you want to publish it. Either revenge this wrong or quit And let our shame die silently.
Crespo	No. Now I hold authority I cannot do what I would do But only what I'm obliged to: Honour must be won legally.

[*Exit* ISABEL]

[*To* INES]
Please put my rod and robes away.

[Exit INES *with rod and robes]*
It's not the sort of case in which
Everyone ends up glad and rich.
Somebody's going to die today.

Don Lope   *[Off]*
Stop! Stop!

Crespo   What's that? Who can it be
Making that damned unholy din
At my door, and then marching in?

[Enter DON LOPE*]*

Don Lope   Pedro Crespo, damn it, it's me!
I'd ridden miles – right over there –
But then news came, which brought me back
Galloping like a maniac –
A very serious affair.
You asked me to come back, you see,
And since we're now good friends, I'm here.

Crespo   God bless you sir, I'll volunteer
To be your host eternally.

Don Lope   Your son didn't turn up. Why not?

Crespo   I'll tell you soon, Don Lope. First
Tell me the reason why you burst
Into the house like that and what
Emergency's occurred to bring
You back so soon. You're tired and tense.

Don Lope   It's a case of such insolence
As is beyond imagining.
It is the worst tomfoolery . . .
Petty officials! I'm tongue-tied!
A sergeant stopped me on my ride
And this is what he said to me . . .
I'm much too angry. You can tell.

Crespo   Go on.

Don Lope   The nerve! The damned disgrace!
The jumped-up Mayor of this place
Has thrown my Captain in a cell.
Great God! My damn leg hurts me so
That, like a woman, I could sob.
Without that damned insistent throb

I'd have arrived here hours ago.
Where can I catch that Mayor tonight,
Crespo? Jesus Christ, I pray
That I may flagellate and flay
This presumptuous parasite.
I'll give his skin to the brigade.

Crespo You've come back to Zalamea
On a wild goose chase, for the mayor
Won't let himself be flogged or flayed.

Don Lope Then, without the Mayor's assistance,
I'll flay the Mayor.

Crespo   Now it's a fact
Everyone would oppose that act.
You'd meet very strong resistance.
Your man's jailed. Do you know why?

Don Lope No; but whyever it was done,
Military justice comes from one
Man, and that's me. If needs be, I
Can chop his head off then and there.

Crespo You're not a countryman, my friend.
You don't begin to comprehend
The powers of a small-town Mayor.

Don Lope He's a peasant. What power's he got?

Crespo Peasants are very stubborn, sir.
If he decides your officer
Shall die, he'll give him the garrotte,
By God sir, yes!

Don Lope   By God sir, no!
You're looking at me dubiously.
All right, come with me. We'll go see
This Mayor. Have we far to go?

Crespo Not far at all. No. Very near.

Don Lope Well, come on man. Tell me, by God
Where is this jack-in-office clod
I've sworn to skin alive?

Crespo   I'm here.

Don Lope Almighty God, I might have known.

Crespo Almighty God, that's what I said.

Don Lope	Well, Crespo, what is said is said.
Crespo	Don Lope, what is done is done.
Don Lope	I'll punish this effrontery After you've freed my officer.
Crespo	I'm keeping him a prisoner On charges of great infamy.
Don Lope	You know the Captain's fealty Is to the King, and that his sole Judge is myself?
Crespo	You know he stole My daughter from her family?
Don Lope	Now, Crespo, is it understood My rank makes me the judge, not you?
Crespo	And is this understood by you – He raped my daughter in a wood?
Don Lope	Do you know, you seem like a child Who tries to talk philosophy?
Crespo	Do you know I went on my knees But he would not be reconciled?
Don Lope	I'll ensure you satisfaction, Promising he will make amends.
Crespo	I don't allow my closest friends To act for me. I take action.
Don Lope	Crespo, come on, let's have the key. I want that Captain right away.
Crespo	The trial's already under way, The evidence –
Don Lope	– What would that be?
Crespo	Some sheets of paper, each one signed, Which I'm examining so I'll Know all I need know at the trial.
Don Lope	I'll take the Captain –
Crespo	– I don't mind If you go to the prison gate, But no further. I've men on guard

                     Posted all around the prison yard.
                     They have guns. And they shoot straight.

Don Lope   I'm used to facing cannon-shot,
                     Under fire twice a week, I'd say,
                     So don't you worry. Anyway,
                     What can I lose now? Not a lot.
                     – Hey soldier! Yes, you! Can you fly?
                     Those troops who marched off up the track –
                     Get after them – order them back –
                     The whole lot – every company.
                     Tell them to march down the main street
                     Ready to fight at any time.
                     Cannon loaded, and muskets primed.
                     Tell them to march to the drum's beat.

Soldier   Sir, you don't have to call them back.
                     They heard the news – then, about turn!
                     They double back here and they'll burn
                     The place down if you say Attack.

Don Lope   Now, God Almighty, it's begun!
                     You'll give our Captain back to us!

Crespo   God Almighty, before he does,
                     I'll go and do what must be done.

                     [*Exeunt* ALL]

                                   ◇

                     [*Outside the prison. Drums beating, off.* DON LOPE,
                     SOLDIERS *heard from outside*]

                     [*Enter* CRESPO, CLERK *and armed* FARMERS]

Don Lope   [*Off*]
                     This is the prison, men. In here
                     Your Captain's shamefully confined.
                     Either he's handed over now
                     Or – burn this prison to the ground
                     And, if the peasants dare resist –
                     Burn down the whole damn town as well.

Clerk   Now they couldn't free him if they
                     Blew up the gates and broached the walls.

Soldier	[*Off*] Kill the peasants! Kill the peasants!
Crespo	Is that the worst thing you can do – Kill the peasants?
Don Lope	Break down the gates! Quick! They've got reinforcements now! Break down the gates!

[*Enter* DON LOPE *and* SOLDIERS. *Enter, between the two parties, the* KING]

King	What's happening? Why does the King of Spain receive Such a strange welcome? Don Lope?
Don Lope	It's the result, Your Majesty, Of the world's most stubborn peasant Transformed into a damn devil. Almighty God! Your Majesty Were it not for your arrival There would have been a fine bonfire To welcome you – this town in flames!
King	Explain, more calmly.
Don Lope	A Captain Of my regiment is in chains. He was arrested by the Mayor Who would not hand him over when I demanded him.
King	Who's this Mayor?
Crespo	I am.
King	Explain what you have done.
Crespo	Here is the evidence, in which Is proved a capital offence. The accused carried off a girl, Raped her in a deserted place And then refused to marry her Although entreated to consent By her father.
Don Lope	This man is both The Mayor and father of the girl.

Crespo	That's true, but it's irrelevant.
	In such a case, if anyone
	Came to me with the same complaint
	Wouldn't I do him justice? Yes.
	Aren't I allowed to do the same
	For my own daughter as I would
	For anybody else's child? Of course.
	Apart from that, just now I jailed
	My own son – so it's obvious
	I'm an impartial magistrate,
	Uninfluenced by claims of blood.
	Here are the legal documents:
	If anyone finds a falsehood
	Or an irregularity
	Or that I've bribed my witnesses
	Or altered their testimony,
	Then I'm content that you should take
	And execute me.
King	He's guilty.
	This evidence has damning weight.
	But you have no authority
	To carry out the sentence, this
	Man must be surrendered to
	The military authorities –
	They'll deal with him.
Crespo	Your Majesty,
	That's just not possible. We have
	Only one court in this small town.
	Whatever verdict that court gives,
	That court imposes. The sentence
	Has already been carried out.
King	What do you mean?
Crespo	You don't believe
	I'm telling you the whole truth, sir?
	If you would like to see him now –
	The Captain's sitting in that chair.

[*The* CAPTAIN *is revealed in a chair, garrotted*]

King	You dared do this?
Crespo	Sire, you confirmed
	The sentence on this man was fair
	Therefore the action that I took
	Cannot have been a bad idea.

King	Surely you'd trust an army court To deal out justice just as boldly?

Crespo I see the justice of the King
As one undivided body.
One body, but with many hands.
Is it important if this man
Was killed by this hand, when the job
Belonged, legally, to that one?
Should a great harvest of the truth
Be burned because of one bad grain?

King Suppose I grant that. But he was
A Captain and a nobleman.
As such, beheading was his right,
Yet you garrotted him?

Crespo   I did.
No nobleman around these parts
Recently has been beheaded.
They're all so very well-behaved.
We've got a block, we've got an axe,
But no bad lords to practice on.
The Captain may make, if he likes,
A plea that we disposed of him
Unworthily, until he does
We'll have to wait. The plea must come
From the plaintiff, not one of us.

King Don Lope, what is done is done.
The death sentence was justified.
There's been an error – it was small.
For the most part, Crespo did right.
Allow no soldier to remain
In Zalamea. It's my will
That we should march this afternoon
On the high road to Portugal.
I appoint you the permanent
Mayor of this town and magistrate.

Crespo Only you, sire, would recognise
My kind of law and honour it.

[*Exit the* KING *and his following*]

Don Lope Crespo, thank your lucky stars
His Majesty arrived in time.

Crespo	Damn it, if he'd never turned up, It'd still be too late for <u>him</u>. [*Indicating the* CAPTAIN]
Don Lope	Wouldn't it have been sensible To have surrendered me the man So I could make him marry her To save her honour?
Crespo	Her good name Is safe. She has chosen to go Into a convent. She marries one Who does not care whether she is Of peasant stock or nobly born.
Don Lope	Give me the other prisoners back.
Crespo	Fetch out that soldier and his page.
	[REBOLLEDO *and* CHISPA *are brought in*]
Don Lope	Better produce your son as well. Juan is already in my pay And mustn't stop in jail.
Crespo	I want To punish him for the attack He made upon the Captain, though He did it for his honour's sake.
Don Lope	Pedro Crespo, that's real justice. I'll make sure that your boy behaves. Call him.
Crespo	He's here.
	[*Enter* JUAN]
Juan	[*To* DON LOPE] Sir, at your feet I kneel, eternally your slave.
Rebolledo	If I live to be a hundred I'll never sing another note.
Chispa	I'll sing each time I remember The instruments that jail has got.
Crespo	And so this old, true story ends. For its shortcomings – pardon, friends.
	[*The End*]

Life's a Dream

This version of *Life's a Dream* was first performed at The Other Place, Stratford-upon-Avon on 23 November 1983 with the following cast:

Rosaura, a confused woman	Barbara Kellermann
Clarion, a foolish servant	Anthony O'Donnell
Sigismund, Prince of Poland	Miles Anderson
Clotaldo, His Keeper	David Waller
Astolfo, Duke of Muscovy	Christopher Neame
Estrella, Princess of Poland	Lesley Duff
Basilio, King of Poland	Charles Kay
Soldiers, Courtiers, Servants	Jeremy Wilkin
	Richard Garnett
	David Killick
	Cyril Nri
Musicians	Michael Tubbs
	Bryan Allen
	Peter Hopkins
	Clifford Pick
Director	John Barton
Designer	Christopher Morley
Lighting	Leo Leibovici
Music	Guy Woolfenden
Voice work	Cicely Berry
	David Carey
Music Director	Michael Tubbs
Design Assistant	Jill Jowett
Stage Manager	Titus Grant
Deputy Stage Manager	Helen Lovat-Fraser
Assistant Stage Manager	Peter Miller

Based on literal versions by Lucy Woolley and Gwenda Pandolfi.

Act One

Scene 1

[*A stage. Enter* ROSAURA *dressed as a man. She mounts a hobby horse and rides gently. Drums and trumpets sound suddenly and the horse neighs and goes wild. She tries to control it but it careers round the stage. She falls off.*]

Rosaura   You're not a horse,
You're a hippogriff.
Why have you thrown me?
Coward, you shied and bucked
At a shadow, a nothing.
Flash without flame!
Fish without scales!
Bird without feathers!
You threw me on these rocks.
Stay in the mountains then:
Make friends with the wolves.
But what about me?
I'm lost . . .
Somewhere in Poland.
Somewhere in the mountains.
I'm a stranger.
I am tired from riding,
The sun is going down
And I've nobody for company
But Clarion the Clown.

[*Enter* CLARION]

Clarion   So this is Poland. What a place.
About as friendly as outer space.
Up there black crags, down there a gloomy lake.
I'm hungry and thirsty and my shoulders ache.

Rosaura   Trouble breeds trouble. We must endure it.

Clarion   A hogshead of wine is the best way to cure it.
Why did we leave our Muscovite nest
To trudge round Europe on some crazy quest?

Rosaura   You know very well
Why we've come to Poland:

                       To find my lost father
                       And win back my honour.

Clarion   [*Sings*] I never had a father
                       But if I had have done
                       I'm sure he would have told me:
                       "Be a man of honour, son."

                       So I rose up one morning
                       And hurried to the fair,
                       For I had heard the rumour
                       That the folk sold honour there.

                       As I walked through the fairground
                       My heart was struck by fear.
                       I heard a giant shouting
                       "Come and buy your honour here."

                       I asked him for some honour.
                       He laughed and turned away,
                       Said: "Honour is expensive
                       Son, are you prepared to pay?

                       "You pay your legs, your eyesight,
                       Your land, your house, your wife,
                       Your sanity, your children
                       And your money and your life."

                       I told him: "Keep your honour:
                       I don't want to be dead."
                       So I went and found a tavern
                       And I bought some wine instead.

Rosaura   Clarion, look there;
                       Look . . . do you see?
                       A tower hewn out of massive blocks
                       Lies at the centre of a maze of rocks
                       Like a chunk hewn out of solid midnight,
                       Or a great mill for grinding sunlight:
                       A tower darker than darkness.

                       [*Sound of chains*]

Clarion   Rosaura. Listen. Clanking.

Rosaura   I can't move. I'm freezing.
                       I can't move. I'm burning.

Sigismund   [*Cries out within*]
                       I am unhappy.

Clarion	Let us leave this tower.
Rosaura	Look. A flickering. A gleam In the blackness. Shifting, shimmering. There's a man, a wild man, In a tomb there or a dungeon. Let's hear what he has to say.

[SIGISMUND *comes forward, chained. He is carrying a picture-book*]

Sigismund	What have I done that I should suffer so? What crime have I committed? Tell me, stars. I have been born. Is that a crime in men? Were other men not born as I was born? Yet they are blessed and I have here no blessings.

[*Turns over the pages of the book*]

A bird is born, a swallow,
Little and damp and shaken,
It grows so bright and dark and feathery,
A spray of flowers on the wing.
It slices through the air so speedily
That it outflies imagining
And leaves its nest forsaken.
Then why can't I
Be like a swallow flying free?

[*He turns the page to a picture of a salmon*]

A fish is born, a salmon.
Child of the waterfall's rock and sprays.
Its rainbow armour fitting perfectly,
It cuts the oceans like a knife,
Charting and measuring the sea
And all the million forms of life
In the vast cold waterways.
Then why can't I
Be like a salmon swimming free?

[*He turns the page to a picture of a waterfall*]

A spring is born, a stream,
Welling up among grass to go
As serpents travel, swift and windingly.
The river sings its silver thanks
And joys in its mobility
To flowers and beasts along its banks

As they watch its dazzling flow.
Then why can't I
Be like a river, flowing free?

[*He turns to a picture of a leopard*]

A beast is born, a leopard,
Delicate as a hyacinth.
Its shaven hide is dappled cunningly
With paintbrush marks of black and gold.
But the grown leopard shows a cruelty
That's natural, so we are told,
A monster in a labyrinth.
Then why, why, can't I
Be like a leopard running free?

Born out of rage,
Eaten with rage,
I'm a volcano. Watch me bleed.
Give me a knife – I'll show you surgery
And wrench out, raggedy and raw
Bits of my heart. Captivity!
So is there some reason or some law
Denies me the one thing I need,
Which God gave swallows and salmon too,
And beasts and leopards: to be free?

Rosaura	What a sad story.
Sigismund	Who's that? I can't see. Clotaldo, is it you?
Clarion	Go on, say it is, But don't mention me.
Rosaura	We are travellers Lost in this ravine We heard your sorrow.
Sigismund	So you know I'm weak? Then you must die.
Clarion	Would you repeat that? I didn't quite hear. I'm a little bit deaf in my right ear.
Sigismund	I'll tear you both in pieces.
Rosaura	I kneel. If you are human I know that you will spare us. We are humble creatures.

Sigismund	Your voice is gentle. When I look on you I find that I grow soft. You trouble me. Who are you? O I know the world so little, For I have spent my whole life in this prison, If how I am is living. Since my birth I have known nothing but this wilderness Where I have lived alone, a living dead thing. Till now I never spoke to anyone But one old man who listens to my sorrows And teaches me rare words and how to name things, And tells me tales about the earth and sky. But till today no one has calmed my anger, O you have eased my eyes and charmed my ears, For you refresh me and you make me wonder.
Rosaura	I do not know how I should answer you. I'm full of wonder too . . . What shall I say? Did Heaven lead me here To see someone unhappier than myself? I cannot tell and yet I think it must be. There was a wise man once who lived on herbs: "Can there be anyone," he asked himself, "More poor and sad than I?" And then he saw Another wise man picking up the leaves That he had thrown away. He found his answer. And so have I, for I have been complaining Of this bad world, and you have answered me. For what I think of as unhappiness You would call joy, as if you picked my leaves up. Then if you can find comfort from my sorrows Take them and let me tell you who I am.

[*Enter* CLOTALDO. *He fires a shot*]

Clotaldo	Guards! Soporific cowards! There are intruders in the tower.
Clarion	More trouble.
Sigismund	That's Clotaldo. He's my jailer.
Clotaldo	Place them under strict arrest And cut them down if they resist.

[*Enter* GUARDS *with masked faces*]

Clarion	I'm a completely lovable clown. I'll be very cut up if you cut me down.

Clotaldo	The King of Poland has decreed This a forbidden place And that the penalty is death To see this monster's face. Surrender to the guard Of the tower by the lake Or my pistol will tear out your throats Like a sudden snake.
Sigismund	Do not harm them, master. You'll all die if you do, For with my nails and teeth I will fight with you.
Clotaldo	Sigismund, remember your own fate When you threaten homicide, Heaven has decreed When you were born, you died. Remember this prison Is a curb upon your pride. Lock the tower door And take him back inside.
Sigismund	Yes, heavens, you are right to steal my freedom. If I was free I'd rise up like a giant And pile up stones and make a staircase mountain And batter down the windows of the sun.
Clotaldo	Perhaps your present sufferings are meant To stop you doing just that. Away with him.

[*Guards take* SIGISMUND *out*]

Surrender to the guards.

Rosaura	Here is my sword. I surrender it to you. I will not yield it Into less noble hands.
Clarion	<u>My</u> sword's a bit bent And blunt at the end. It's a prize for a booby: Here you are, friend.

[CLARION *gives the sword to a* GUARD. CLOTALDO *takes* ROSAURA'S. GUARD *takes* CLARION *out.*]

Rosaura	If I must die, sir, Please guard it well. It holds some great secret: It is a legacy From my lost father.
Clotaldo	And who was he?
Rosaura	I never knew him, But I trust his sword, And so I came to Poland, For revenge on a man Who has wronged my honour.

[CLOTALDO *takes his mask off*]

Clotaldo	[*Aside*] What is this, heavens? I am flabbergasted. All my own confusions, My shame and my sorrows Swamp my heart and mind. Who gave it to you?
Rosaura	My mother.
Clotaldo	Her name?
Rosaura	I cannot tell you that.
Clotaldo	[*Aside*] Heaven help me! Can this be Illusion or reality? This is the sword I gave to my sweet love When I was living still in Muscovy. I swore that whosoever wore that sword Would find me kind as if he was my son. I am bewildered. Stranger, do not think You are alone in your misfortunes here. You must go in but I will use you gently.

[*Exit* ROSAURA]

He has her eyes, as hot as shooting stars.
Now am I like a man locked in a room
Who hears a sound in the street and runs to the window.
My heart flies out of my eyes to stare at him.
I'm weeping. He's my son. What shall I do?
Let's work it out. One, he has offered me
My own good sword to win favour. Two,
By coming here he's brought his death day with him.

What must I do? O heavens, what must I do?
Take him before the King? That's certain death.
Hide him? I cannot, I should break my oath.
Now is it with me as in some old tale:
On one side, love, on one side, loyalty.
I'm torn. But why? I should not hesitate.
For loyalty to kings is more than life
And more than honour. I believe that's true,
So do not mock me. What was it he said?
He came here to avenge some injury.
To leave an insult unavenged is shameful.
That is our code. Honour's so delicate,
A little breath, a puff of wind can smear it.
He is my son, my blood is in his veins:
What shall I do? I'll seek some middle way.
In this bad world that's best. I'll tell the King
This boy is mine. My loyalty may move him.
Then I can help him to avenge his honour.
But if the King is cruel, my son must die.
What's the worst fate the gods can give?
Some say to die, but others say . . . to live.

Scene 2

[*Dawn. Drums and trumpets. Enter on one side* ASTOLFO, DUKE OF
MUSCOVY, *attended, and on the other side* PRINCESS ESTRELLA, *also
attended*]

Astolfo   Estrella! Star-girl! Princess! Empress! Queen!
Your eyes are bright as comets. Drums and trumpets
Greet you and mix their homage with sweet nature.
Look how the birds and fountains blend their music
And all things wonder that behold your face.
Trumpets made of feathers, birds of brass
And the rough cannons hail you as their queen.
The birds cry out, "Look, that is bright Aurora",
The trumpets, that Athene's here, the flowers
That you are Flora. O you mock the day
Even as the bright day mocks the banished night.
You are the dawn, Aurora, as you shine,
Athene as you war, in peace sweet Flora,
And all in all you are my proud heart's queen.

Estrella   If deeds prove words, you will be proved a liar.
You do me wrong to flatter me, Astolfo.

	Your courteous, amorous vocabulary And your display of military might Do not quite blend. Your silver tongue talks love But in your mind you dream of iron power.
Astolfo	No, you are wrong to doubt my faith, Estrella. Fair cousin hear me out. Basilio Is King of Poland and a widower. He is old now (Time mocks us all with age) And more inclined to study than to women. He has no child, so we both claim the throne . . .
Estrella	I am the daughter of his eldest sister.
Astolfo	It's true I am the youngest sister's son, For I was born to her in Muscovy, Yet, being a man, I must take precedence. This has been argued with our uncle King Who says he means to reconcile us both, And he has fixed this day and place to do it. And that is why I've come from Muscovy. Not to make war, though you make war on me With all the weapons of your loveliness, But to make love and win you, my Estrella. If we two marry, Poland will be strong.
Estrella	My heart thanks yours for your kind courtesy. Yet I am only partly satisfied: There is a picture hanging round your neck Which rather gives the lie to what you say. Do not confuse your longings for the throne With other nicer longings of your own.
Astolfo	I'll satisfy you fully as to that . . .

[*Drums and trumpets sound*]

But may not do so now. The King is coming.

[*Enter* KING BASILIO, *attended*]

O most wise King . . .

Estrella	O learned King . . .
Astolfo	Who rules Among the stars . . .
Estrella	The galaxies . . .

Astolfo   The heavens . . .

Estrella   You plot the star-paths . . .

Astolfo   Trace their fiery footsteps.

Estrella   You hear their music . . .

Astolfo   And you read their meaning . . .

Estrella   O let me kneel before your royal feet.

Astolfo   O let me press my lips upon your hand.

Basilio   Dutiful nephew, loving niece, embrace me.
You come in love and hope. However high
Your wishes soar you shall be satisfied.
So clear your minds of that, and all be silent.
Brave peers of Poland, vassals, kinsmen, friends.
You know already that for my deep wisdom
I am surnamed the Learned by the world,
And in defiance of Time's dusty heel
Painters and sculptors all around the globe
Create star-glowing images of me,
Which will outlive by tens of centuries
This fading face, these failing bones, this flesh:
Basilio the Learned. And the Great.
You know the science that I love the most:
The mathematics, by the means of which
I make a fool of Fate and cheat old Time,
Whose function is to unfold Fate itself.
I am the canny duellist who so far
Has always made the winning thrust. Poor Time,
His every stroke and counter-stroke is marked
Upon my charts ahead of him. I read him.
There are star mountains and I climb their peaks.
There are star forests and I know their paths,
And there are swamps and whirlpools made of stars.
Circles of snow, bright canopies of glass,
Cut by the moon, illumined by the sun,
These crystalline, concentric necklaces
These specks, these beads, these spirals, whirling tear-drops:
These are my life, my study and my passion,
These are my books, their diamond lettering
Printed upon bright sapphire-paper pages
By the great golden printing-press of Heaven.
I turn one blue page of the Universe

And, cruel or kind, there is our human future,
Easy to read as a child's alphabet.
And yet I wish, before I'd understood
The universe's simplest syllable,
The stars had poured their poison-fire on me.
A learned man's the victim of his learning.
For he who has foreknowledge of his fate
Murders himself and plays the suicide
In his own story. So perhaps with me.
Be silent still and hear me out with wonder.

I'm old now, but when I was young and fresh
I had a secret and unhappy son
At whose sad birth there was high rage in heaven.
Before the warm grave of his mother's womb
Transmitted him into the yellow daylight
(For birth and death are very much alike)
His mother dreamed a child monstrosity
Smeared with her life's blood, burst out of her entrails,
Took life and was her death. And when the day
Came for his birth, this omen was proved true:
In my experience, omens always are.
The sun was red as blood and fought the moon.
They took our planet as their wrestling-ground;
Silver and gold grappled and interlocked.
It was the greatest and most terrible
Of all the eclipses that the sun has suffered
Since it wept blood, mourning the death of Christ.
There was no star-fire in the firmament.
Palaces shook. And Sigismund was born.
He tore his mother's life out and so showed
His nature to the world as if to say,
"I repay good with evil. I'm a man."

I knew then he would grow up to be vicious.
A cruel prince and a despotic King;
That Poland would be torn by civil war
And that his wildness would debauch the Kingdom
Into a foul academy of chaos.
I knew he'd strike me down and use my beard
As if it were a carpet for his boots.
Who'd not believe such omens? I decided
That I must cage the beast and find out whether
One cunning King could overcome the stars.

I gave out that my son had died at birth.
I built a tower among night-black boulders
In a ravine beyond the reach of daylight,
And that is where he lives. The penalty
For trespassers is death without a trial.
He sees and talks with no one but Clotaldo
Who tutors him in science and religion
And is the only witness of his woes.

Three things must now be thought on. Pray you, mark me.
One, I love Poland and I won't allow her
To be oppressed or crushed by tyranny.
Two, Christian charity: what right have I
To keep my son from that prerogative
Which by divine and human law is his?
Shall I turn criminal because of crimes
Which he has not committed, though he may?
Three, what if I have been too credulous?
What if he's gentle? The most cruel star
Can influence the will but cannot force it
Because a man's will is a gift from God.

I've wavered and I've weighed this, and I have
Devised a remedy which will amaze you.
I mean to set my son upon my throne
And to invest him with my royal power,
And you must all obey him as your King.
This stratagem can lead us to three outcomes
Which complement the three points I have made.
One, if he's prudent, wise and kind and gentle
And gives the lie to what is prophesied,
Then you shall have him as your own true King.
Two, if he proves reckless and cruel and wild
My moral obligation's at an end,
And it will seem in me a kind of mercy
To reimprison him, not punishment
But justice. Three, if that should be the outcome
I will ensure the Polish throne shall be
By you two occupied illustriously.
This, as I am your King, I now command
And, as I am his father, I require
And, as I am a wise man, I advise it,
And, as I'm old, I tell you blunt and plain.
And last, if Kings be slaves to their own kingdoms,
I, as your humble slave, beseech you all.

Astolfo	Justice herself could form no plan more fair.
Estrella	God save the Prince and let him be your heir.
Astolfo	Long live Basilio.
Estrella	God save the King.
All	Long live Basilio. God save the King.

[*Music. Exit all but* BASILIO]

Basilio
I thank you for listening.
We shall learn tomorrow
Whether my son shall be a King
Or whether he'll bring sorrow.

[*Enter* CLOTALDO *with* ROSAURA *and* CLARION *chained and blindfolded.*]

Clotaldo
A word, sire.

Basilio
Clotaldo. You are always welcome.
What's wrong?

Clotaldo
My lord, a grievous thing has happened,
Though in a sense it is a joyful thing . . .

Basilio
Go on.

Clotaldo
These two young men have seen the prince.
They got into the tower . . .

Basilio
Don't fret, Clotaldo.
Since I have publicly proclaimed the truth,
Discovering the secret is no crime.
Attend me in an hour. I've much to tell you,
And you will have a busy day tomorrow,
For you must help me with the strangest act
The planet earth has seen. As for your prisoners,
I will forgive you for your negligence.
Unbind their arms and eyes. You are all pardoned.

[*Exit*]

Clotaldo
God save the King
And may he live for ever! Heaven is kind.
I thought it would be hard but it was easy.
[*Aside*] I will not tell him that he is my son.
I did his mother wrong, and if he knew me
I fear he'd hate me. Strangers, you are free.

Rosaura	I kiss your feet, your grace.
Clarion	I'll kiss you any place.
Rosaura	You saved my life.
Clarion	I'll be your slave forever.
Clotaldo	Get up, both of you. [*To* CLARION] Don't try to be clever.
Clarion	I'm trying to be foolish.
Clotaldo	You've succeeded.
Clarion	Why, then I'll be outside if I am needed.
Clotaldo	If needed I'll give you a clarion call.
Clarion	Sir, you could be the biggest fool of them all.

[*Exit* CLARION]

Rosaura   You saved my life . . .

Clotaldo   You have no life. You say you have been wronged,
But noble men have neither life nor honour
Until they are avenged. [*Aside*] I see that I
Must educate the boy. Sure, this will move him.

Rosaura   I am not ashamed. I have done nothing wrong.

Clotaldo   Honour's not what you do
But what is done to you.
You can wash your face
If it's splashed with mud
But honour can only
Be washed with blood.
A man without honour's a mongrel pup
Snapping at fleas. [*Aside*] That should stir him up.

Rosaura   I will avenge my honour
And so win life.

Clotaldo   Well said.
Take back your sword.
Vow vengeance on your enemy.
That sword was mine
(I mean it was, just now)
It will serve you well:
Use it like a man.

Rosaura	Then in your name I gird it on again And swear as I am man To be revenged on him Who has wronged my honour.
Clotaldo	And I will likewise swear on oath to help you.
Rosaura	You would not say so if you knew his name.
Clotaldo	Have I not sworn it? Is it some great man?
Rosaura	So great, I dare not tell you who he is. I fear to lose your favour.
Clotaldo	No, you'd win it If you would trust me.
Rosaura	No, I dare not tell you.
Clotaldo	If only I could find out who he is. Tell me his name. I am your friend. You need me.
Rosaura	I trust you. You shall know my enemy Is great Astolfo, Duke of Muscovy.
Clarion	[Aside] Why, this is worse than I thought possible. I must learn more of this. Let us examine This carefully. You are a Muscovite. Therefore Astolfo is your natural lord. And therefore he cannot have wronged your honour. Quench this mad ardour.
Rosaura	Though he is my prince, He's wronged me.
Clotaldo	No, a prince can do no wrong, Not even if he struck you in the face.
Rosaura	My wrong was worse than that.
Clotaldo	Then tell it me.
Rosaura	I am not what I seem, This is show, disguise, a costume. My name is Rosaura. [Lets down her hair] I had a noble mother In the court of Muscovy. A deceiver wooed and won her.

I do not know his name
For she would never tell me,
But I think he was valiant
Because I sometimes feel
His courage in myself.
He told her the old story:
He'd be true to her,
He would marry her.
But one day he left her:
She was too low-born
For his nobility.
From this loose knot
I came into the world,
And so in time her tale
Was told again in me.
Astolfo is the man
Who despoiled my honour.
He swore he'd marry me
And for a little while
I thought I was happy.
Suddenly he left.
He came here to Poland
To marry his Estrella.
As a star first joined us
So a star destroyed us.
I wept within.
I was mocked,
I was angry,
I was mad,
I was dead,
I was . . . me . . .
Babel . . . Muddle . . . Hell.

Pain is felt, not words
But my mother understood.
When you know the person
To whom you tell your weakness
Has been weak herself,
It's as if you are both lost
In the same strange country.
That is a comfort.
She said, "Go to Poland,
Either make him marry you
Or kill him. Kill him with

Your father's sword."
I swore that.

She dressed me as a man
And said, "Show this sword
To the noble men in Poland,
One of them will know it
And be kind to you
Because you are his child."

I want to meet my father
And tell him how I hate him.
It is because of him
That my Astolfo left me.
He said he could not marry
A girl who had no father
And did not know his name.
Hate is a clear thing.
Though I am in the darkness
I am clear about my father.

Clotaldo   [*Aside*] O what a maze. I don't know what to do.
My honour's gored. Astolfo's powerful.
He is my overlord, she just a woman.
She must not know yet that I am her father,
For then she would compel me to avenge her.
That is our code. Besides she loves me now.
That's sweet to me. Best leave it as it is.
I don't know what to do or what to say,
Best to say nothing till I find my way.

Rosaura   Why do I feel such trust and fondness for you?
I think it is because you are kind and gentle.
Why are you silent?

Clotaldo   You have sworn two oaths;
One of revenge and blood and one to win
Your love Astolfo. These oaths are at odds.
I think that is because you do not know
Whether you love or hate him.

Rosaura   Both.

Clotaldo   That's common.
But I believe your oaths are dreams, Rosaura.
You cannot marry one of such high blood.
You must accept that.

Rosaura	I have tried to do so. I locked my rage within but it will out. Damn his fine phrases, damn his gentle smiling. Damn his sweet kisses, his fumblings and his fondlings. I'll cut his lying throat. How dare he leave me?
Clotaldo	You are violent because you have been hurt, But Time will mend that. For the good of Poland The Duke must wed Estrella. He must do it.
Rosaura	I will prevent him.
Clotaldo	How?
Rosaura	I do not know.
Clotaldo	Do you still hope to win his love again?
Rosaura	I cannot tell.
Clotaldo	Well, you will never win him Unless you put a dress on.
Rosaura	I'll not do that.
Clotaldo	You must. As you are now you are immodest, Unnatural, and, which is worst, unreal. You are very fair.
Rosaura	My hair is foul and matted.
Clotaldo	There, you are a woman.
Rosaura	I will put a dress on But I will keep my oath.
Clotaldo	I don't believe you.
Rosaura	The only man I'll marry is Astolfo.
Clotaldo	We will speak further. For the present time Since you are unhappy it's not good for you To be alone. Therefore I will contrive That you shall serve Estrella.
Rosaura	I can't do that.
Clotaldo	We often think we cannot when we can, And what we think we can we often cannot.
Rosaura	You must not make me break my oath Or go against my honour.

Clotaldo	We'll speak further. I must attend the King on some great purpose. Go in Rosaura, and put on a dress.

[*Exit* CLOTALDO. ROSAURA *takes off the rest of her disguise. As she does so she sings.*]

Rosaura	Dreamed I was the lover Of a beautiful thief But when I woke up I was a shipwreck on a reef. Dreamed that I was happy Or so it seemed to seem. My lover smiled Just like a clown in a dream.

A clown in a dream,
A clown in a dream
I had a dream
I was a clown in a dream.
A clown in a dream
Falling upside down,
And when I woke up,
I was a dream in a clown.

[*Exit* ROSAURA]

Act Two

Scene 1

[*Enter* KING BASILIO *and* CLOTALDO]

Clotaldo   Your orders, sire, have all been carried out.

Basilio   Tell me, Clotaldo.

Clotaldo   I went back to the tower
And had a pleasant sleeping draft prepared;
A blend of certain rare and powerful herbs,
Whose secret strength lays waste the human mind
So that the victim becomes numb to pain,
And at the last is like a living corpse.

Basilio   Sweet medicine is so full of Nature's secrets
That there's no plant nor animal nor stone
That does not have rare powers or properties.
For if the matchless malice of mankind
Can find a thousand poisons, is it strange
That violent drugs, if they be checked and tempered,
Can bring us sleep, not death? It's palpable.

Clotaldo   I took this drink down to the Prince's cell
And talked a little with him of the arts
And sciences, which he had learned from birds,
From beasts and fishes, mountains and clouds and me.
To raise his spirits to your enterprise
I made him watch a fiery-feathered eagle,
Flying through tree-tall flames of gold and white,
Winging beyond the clouded, lower skies,
Soaring up high into the land of the sun.
Until he turned into a shooting star,
A feathered ray of streaming gilded light.
I praised that bright adventurer and said,
"The eagle is the King of all the birds,
The undisputed lord." This image spurred him
To speak of sovereignty. Ambitiously
And proudly too his heart began to stir
Heroically. He said: "It is amazing
Within the airy Kingdom of the birds
One bird holds sway. So many citizens
And yet they all seem happy to obey.

But I'm a subject through some fault of birth,
And, were I free, I never could become
Subject to any man on earth."

Basilio   So, he was roused.

Clotaldo   And so I thought it good
To offer him the potion, and he took it.
No sooner had it trickled down his throat
Than he turned grey as lead. If I'd not known
The drug's effects I'd have supposed him dead.
We brought him to your room, to your own bed.
When he awakes they'll clothe him in your robes
And serve him as they'd serve Your Majesty.

Basilio   You have done well, Clotaldo. Now all is ready.

Clotaldo   Your Highness, if my long obedient years
Have earned, forgive me, any kind of pay,
Will you explain why you have had the Prince
Brought to the palace in this curious way?

Basilio   Your curiosity is just, Clotaldo.
The stars, it is the stars above that threaten
Innumerable tragedies of blood.
I want to test them, yes, test out heaven.
I must discover if his destiny
(However scientifically correct)
May not in fact be slightly mitigated
Or even conquered. I believe a man
Is master of his stars. I wish to try him.
I mean to tell him that he is my son
That I may know his nature. You'll ask why
He was brought here asleep. I'll answer that.
If he should learn today that he's my son
And if he then proves cruel and so tomorrow
Awakes in prison, will he not despair?
Therefore I have contrived a kind of ease.
I'll make him think that it is all a dream.
Thus I'll discover his true character,
For he will act by instinct when he wakes.
And, if he fails he'll have some consolation;
For if one day he's worshipped as a King,
The next flung back into his dungeon den,
He will be able to believe he dreamed it.
And that's a useful, realistic creed:
To live life is a dream indeed.

Clotaldo	I believe you are mistaken, sire, To embark on this experiment. But as the subject is awake There's no time now for argument.
Basilio	I will withdraw. Stay here: you are his tutor. Tell him the truth. Don't let him be bewildered But help him clear his mind.
Clotaldo	Am I to tell him Everything?
Basilio	Yes, for if he knows the truth He may succeed and pass the test I've set him. I'll send the Duke and Princess to him also, So all the court shall shortly test my son. A danger known is often not a danger, And so it will be with Sigismund.

[*Exit* BASILIO. *Enter* CLARION *in court livery*]

Clarion	I've come to see King Basil's play. To get in his theatre I've had to pay: One glass of beer to a growling guard, Two chops to the dogs in the Palace yard, Three rings to a chambermaid – real imitation – In exchange for some curious information. Four tots of rum and a barrel of beer To a royal red-nosed halberdier. Five silk gowns, ornate and oriental To a lady-in-waiting who's sentimental. That's what I paid, but what have I bought? An under-flunkey's position at court. Where I am guaranteed a ringside view Of the Royal Circus of How D'Ye Do, With performing Princesses, Kings who eat fire, And a Prince walking along the High Wire.
Clotaldo	Good morning, Clarion, What is the news? New clothes I see, But rather strange shoes.
Clarion	Now you've agreed To avenge her offences, My mistress Rosaura Has come to her senses.

You've done so much
To relieve her distress
That she's even put on
A beautiful dress.

Clotaldo I'm glad. Those clothes
Put her sex to shame.

Clarion On top of all that
She's changed her name
To the lady Astraea.
She says she's your niece,
And she's landed a job,
Wonders never cease,
As a lady-in-waiting
To Princess Estrella,
(Which she couldn't have done
If she'd stayed as a feller).

Clotaldo And how does your life
As a court clown feel?

Clarion I'm desperate, sir,
I long for a meal.
A six-course dinner
Is what I deserve
But nobody feeds me.
I've no one to serve.

Clotaldo Then be my servant,
Though the fare is frugal.

Clarion I am your slave, sir.

Clotaldo Then don't blow that bugle.

Clarion I'm full of joy
And I'll learn to diet.

Clotaldo But first you must learn
To try to be quiet.

[*Music*]

Ah, here he comes in princely splendour.

Clarion   Who?

Clotaldo Prince Sigismund, and his royal retinue.

[SIGISMUND *enters, carried on a litter by* SERVANTS, *He wakes up. They help to dress him as he speaks.*]

Sigismund	Stars above . . . what's all this brightness? Stars above . . . am I in a vision? Sigismund, waking in an amazing bed, Flowing with softnesses and shining . . . Sigismund, clothed in robes as light As sunset clouds and shining . . . Sigismund, carried down sunny corridors By silent servants, eyes and faces shining . . . This isn't a dream. I know I am awake. It doesn't make sense, but it's joy. I am as I thought I never would be: My chains are gone. Today I'm free.
1st Servant	How sad he is.
2nd Servant	And wouldn't you be sad If you were him?
Clarion	I wouldn't be.
2nd Servant	What, him?
Clarion	No, sad.
2nd Servant	And yet who would change places with him?
Clarion	Me, for a start.
2nd Servant	We'd better speak to him.
1st Servant	Will you be pleased to hear the Palace choir?
Sigismund	No singing. No.
2nd Servant	For your delight we planned Some songs.
Sigismund	I want a military band.

[*Fanfare*]

This sound is wondrous to my ears:
Now I throw off all doubts and fears.

Clotaldo	Your highness, my dear lord, I kiss your hand and say I'm proud that I may humbly Pay homage thus today.
Sigismund	It is Clotaldo. What's his mind, his meaning? In prison he tormented me but now He treats me with respect. What's happening?

Clotaldo   I understand your wonderment.
In a world where all is strange,
Your mind is full of doubts and fears
Because of this sudden change.
But I can soothe away all doubts
And beat all terrors down.
I'm charged to tell you that you are
Heir to the Polish Crown.
You have been kept away from men
Because astrology
Predicted that your rule as King
Would prove a tyranny.
You have been brought here to defy
What the stars relate,
For the man who is magnanimous
Can triumph over fate.
While you were unconscious
You were brought here to this place.
The King, your father, will tell you the rest
Of your story, face to face.

Sigismund   Traitor: one who betrays.
Traitor, you are my traitor.
Now I know who I am,
I am full of pride.
Because of what I am,
I am full of power.
Traitor to Poland, traitor,
Hiding me away
Like a dirty secret,
Traitor to me, Sigismund,
Your prisoner, your prince . . .

Clotaldo   My lord.

Sigismund   Savage to me and servile to the King.
Therefore the law, the King and I condemn you
To death. I'll execute you with these hands.

1st Servant   My lord . . .

2nd Servant   Your highness . . .

3rd Servant   Sir . . .

Clotaldo   My lord . . .

Sigismund	Out of my way. Nobody stops me, no one. Out of my way, by God, or I will throw you Out of that window down into the lake.
Clarion	It's a dark lake.
1st Servant	Go, sir.
2nd Servant	You'd better go.
Clotaldo	I pity you. How powerful you seem But you may find you're acting in a dream.

[*Exit* CLOTALDO]

2nd Servant	Consider, sir . . .
Sigismund	Get out of here.
2nd Servant	He only obeyed his King.
Sigismund	He should have refused. I was his Prince. To lock me away was an unjust thing.
2nd Servant	It wasn't for him but the King to decide Right from wrong and white from black.
Sigismund	You must dislike yourself very much To risk answering me back.
Clarion	The Prince is right and you are wrong.
2nd Servant	And who asked you to say?
Clarion	Poland's a free country, isn't it?
1st Servant	Who are you, anyway?
Clarion	I'm the world champion busy-body. I've a finger in every pie. I could kill you two birds With one bush if I liked But I've bigger fish to fry.
Sigismund	I know you. You're Clarion the Clown.
Clarion	Local vodka. Chuck it down.

[CLARION *passes* SIGISMUND *the bottle*]

Sigismund	[*Drinks*] I like you, Clarion the Clown. You please me,

	You're the only one I like out of all these.
Clarion	Where pleasing's to be done, It pleases me to please.

[*Enter* ASTOLFO. *He leaves his hat on*]

Astolfo	This is a happy day, most noble prince: This is the day when you, the sun of Poland, Must rise and fill the sky and shed your brightness On our horizons like the blushful dawn, For you have risen like the sunrise does Above the darkness of the dusky mountains. O may the lovely laurels on your brow, These late adornments, flourish long upon you And never wither.
Sigismund	God be with you, sir.
Astolfo	Sir, I forgive you that you do not know me And do not give me honour when it's due. I am Astolfo, Duke of Muscovy, And we are cousins. You and I are equals.
1st Servant	Remember your grace, his highness was brought Up in the mountains, not in the court.
2nd Servant	The Duke, my lord, is an aristocrat.
Sigismund	He bores me. And he won't take off his hat.
1st Servant	His rank allows that.
2nd Servant	More respect is due.
Sigismund	To me, not him. I'm getting tired of you.

[*Enter* ESTRELLA]

Estrella	Sir, welcome to the throne which longs for you And gratefully receives you. May you reign, Confounding fate, and live a thousand years.
Sigismund	Clarion, who is she? Who is this human goddess?
1st Servant	Princess Estrella, sir.
2nd Servant	She is your cousin.
Sigismund	Estrella? That's a star, but I should say She is the sun. I thank you for your kindness.

Queen of the skies, you are the waking daylight.
You could add brightness to the morning star
And light the heavens. When you rise at morning
There's nothing left for the dull sun to do.
O let me kiss your hand, that snow-pure cup
From which the gentle breeze drinks whiteness up.

Estrella   Eloquent Prince, I did not mean . . .

Astolfo   He must not touch her.

2nd Servant   I'll intervene.

1st Servant   Astolfo's angry.

2nd Servant   Sir, is not your greeting
Too ardent and too rough for a first meeting?

Sigismund   Didn't I say keep out of my way?
Didn't I say keep out of my sight?
The coach is coming. Keep off the highway.

2nd Servant   You have just said that rulers must
Always cleave to what is just.

Sigismund   I also said, for Jesus' sake,
That I would throw you in the lake.

2nd Servant   You couldn't sire, a man of my standing . . .

Sigismund   O couldn't I?

Estrella   Stop him!

Sigismund   Happy landings!

[*Lifts him in his arms and rushes out*]

Astolfo   Sweet, fetch the King.

Estrella   I'll ask him to hurry.

Clarion   Tell him I'm here and not to worry.

[*Exit* ESTRELLA. *Re-enter* SIGISMUND]

Sigismund   Your standing notwithstanding, slave,
Rest your bones in that chilly grave.

Astolfo   Restrain yourself, my lord: the difference
Between a beast and man should be as great
As that between a mountain and a palace.

Sigismund	Astolfo, if you carry on Giving advice like that, You'll find you have no stupid head On which to put your stupid hat.

[*Exit* ASTOLFO. *Enter* KING BASILIO]

Basilio   What have you done?

Sigismund   Nothing much. I taught a
Slave a lesson. Dropped him in the water.

[*Pause*]

Are you my father?

Basilio   I am and love you . . .

Sigismund   No, you've done me wrong.

Basilio   You have done wrong, my son. What, take a life
The very first day that you taste your freedom?

Sigismund   He said I couldn't do it, so I did.

Basilio   This grieves me, Prince. Be more intelligent.
I hoped to find a new, wise, prudent man
Triumphing over destiny and the stars.
Instead I find a brutal murderer.
How can I give you love? How can I open
My arms to yours? They are a killer's arms.
I thought to embrace you with a father's love.
But now you'll understand if I prefer
To avoid the arms of a murderer.

Sigismund   I do not want your love or your embraces.
You are a cruel father. You have kept me
Away from you and reared me like a beast.
You have denied my human dignity,
So I feel nothing for you, father. Nothing.

Basilio   I gave you life. I wish I never had.

Sigismund   And if you hadn't, I'd have no complaints.
You gave me life and then wrenched it away.
To give is blessed but give and take away
Is twisted work.

Basilio   Is that the thanks I get
For making a poor prisoner a Prince?

Sigismund	What have you given me that was not mine?
	You took my free will, chained it to the wall,
	And now you are an old, weak dying King,
	And you must leave me everything. It's mine.
	Poland is mine. There's nothing that I owe you.
	You owe me life and happiness and freedom.
	You should be thanking me I do not force you
	To pay your debt.
Basilio	Look on him, everyone:
	See how the stars have kept their promises.
	See, see how cruel and arrogant he is.
	My son, I warn you, be more kind, more gentle,
	More humble. That is good advice to take:
	Perhaps you only dream that you're awake.
Sigismund	Is this a dream? I feel, I hear, I touch.
	I know what I have been and what I am.
	You may regret it but you can't undo it.
	For I am what I am. What's done is done.
	I am half-man, half-beast. I'm not your son.

[*All exit. Enter* ROSAURA *dressed in white*]

Rosaura	Now Sigismund's a prince and I a lady.
	O it is sweet to wear a dress again.
	I'm full of joy. Astolfo loves me still.
	I saw him come to visit his Estrella
	And he still wears my picture. He'd not do that
	Unless he loved me. I will work on him.
	There's time enough to think upon revenge.
	Am I not fair? Am I not painted fine?
	As I am now I'm fit to wed a King.
	A Duke is easy, I will woo and win him.
	Clotaldo says I must not speak to him.
	I owe him much and therefore should obey.
	And yet I will not. I am strong today
	Because I find I'm fairer than Estrella.
	What jewel's best to wear? Or this? Or this?
	I'll find out ways to make myself more fine.
	When I was man my heart was torn by strife.
	But now I'm woman I may yet be wife.

[*She puts on various jewels. Enter* SIGISMUND]

Sigismund	The world is all as I thought it would be.
	Through books and pictures I foresaw it all.

But if I had to wonder at one thing
In this new world, I'd wonder at a woman
And at her beauty. Once in some old book
I read that of all things in God's creation
Man was God's loveliest and noblest work
Because a man is like a little world.
But I believe that woman is the noblest,
For she's a little heaven and more lovely . . .
And far more so, if she's the one I look on.

[ROSAURA *sees* SIGISMUND]

Rosaura   It is the prince. I'll leave him.

Sigismund   Wait, woman, listen, Tell me who you are.

Rosaura   I think, but am not sure, that I have seen you.

Sigismund   I think I've seen your beauty once before.

Rosaura   I've seen your rage and sorrow in your prison.

Sigismund   Who are you? You are fair. I've found my life.

Rosaura   I'm a poor lady in Estrella's train.

Sigismund   No, do not say that. Say you are the sun
And that Estrella is a petty star
Who gets her splendour from your borrowed flame.
O I have seen the kingdom of the flowers
Where every odour is and every hue,
And where the rose is goddess o'er the rest
And queen because she is most beautiful.
And I have seen a world of precious gems
Deep in the dark academy of the mines,
And how the rest all hail the diamond
And call it emperor for its radiance.
And I have seen up in the courts of heaven,
High in the lovely empire of the stars,
The morning star in royal pre-eminence.
And I have seen how in the very spheres
The sun, that is the oracle of day,
Calls up the planets to his parliament
And plays the speaker. If among all these,
The flowers, the mines, the firmament, the planets,
The fairest is exalted, how can I
Serve one who is less beautiful than you,
Who are for loveliness and excellence
The peer of roses, diamonds, sun and stars?

[Enter CLOTALDO, *unseen]*

Clotaldo	*[Aside]* I educated him. It's up to me To advise the boy. But first I'll wait and see.
Rosaura	My lord, I'm honoured by your eloquence But I'm lost for words. My reply is silence.
Sigismund	Your body speaks and everything about you. You shine. O do not leave me in the dark.
Rosaura	I beg your leave to go . . .
Sigismund	Stay where you are. You do not beg my leave, you simply take it.
Rosaura	If you won't give it I am bound to take it.
Sigismund	Well then, you'll see the dark side of my passion, The Beast-man. Say, why are you dressed so fine Unless you mean to set a man on fire?
Rosaura	I did not dress to please you.
Sigismund	But you do. You've made yourself a lure and flame to men.
Rosaura	I have not . . .
Sigismund	Come, resistance poisons patience. I've seen you thus, and seen you as a man. Now I will see you as you truly are.
Rosaura	You would not dare. You will respect my honour.
Sigismund	We'll see. You'll make me try it, though I am Afraid of you because you are so fair. I must know whether I can love or not. I want to conquer the impossible. Today he said I couldn't. Now I'll throw Your chastity out of the window after.

[He throws her on the bed and starts to tear her clothes off.]

Clotaldo	*[Aside]* It is not good that he should thus divest him, And yet the King has said that we must test him.
Rosaura	The stars were right. They spoke the truth. I see You'll be a tyrant. You will fill up Poland With riot, slaughter, treachery and crime. What else can be expected of a creature As barbarous, inhuman and relentless, As is a beast that is brought up with beasts?

Clotaldo	[*Aside*] I've waited long enough and I have seen What he intends. I'd better intervene.
Sigismund	I've tried to speak to you with gentleness Because I hoped you would be kind to me, But since you are so sure I am a beast, I'll prove I am one.
Clotaldo	Pardon me, my lord . . .
Sigismund	How did you get in here?
Clotaldo	I . . .
Sigismund	Go away.
Rosaura	I'm lost. Wait, listen . . .
Sigismund	No, I am a tyrant. I am the Beast-man.
Clotaldo	Wait, my lord. Be careful.
Sigismund	Doddering old fool, how dare you interrupt?
Clotaldo	I heard your voice raised angrily And wanted, Prince, to say: Try to be mild and humble And show gentleness today, Or you may wake to find your power Has melted, like a dream away.
Sigismund	Now I will kill you. We'll soon see If this is a dream or reality.

[CLOTALDO *kneels and grabs hold of him*]

Clotaldo	I mean to live.
Sigismund	Let go.
Clotaldo	I'll not let go. I know you mean to throw me in the lake.
Rosaura	For God's sake help.
Sigismund	Old fool, I say, let go. Or I will crush you in my arms to death.
Rosaura	Quickly, come quickly! Clotaldo's being murdered.

[*Exit* ROSAURA. *Enter* ASTOLFO]

Astolfo	Stay, noble prince. What, stain an old man's blood? You will not do that.

Sigismund	If blood is in his dusty veins, I will.
Astolfo	I'll answer for his life.
Sigismund	You'll answer, will you? You have insulted me. Now I shall kill you.
Astolfo	Then I will draw in self-defence, my lord, And that's no treason.

[*They fight*]

Clotaldo	[*To* ASTOLFO] Do not hurt him, sire.

[*Enter* BASILIO, ESTRELLA, *servants and* CLARION]

Basilio	What, swords?
Estrella	Astolfo, hold.
Basilio	Hold, both of you. What is it?
Astolfo	Nothing. You are here: it's over.

[ASTOLFO *sheathes his sword*]

No man will draw his sword before his king.

Sigismund	You should have said you drew against your King.
Clotaldo	Humour him, sire. Do it all gently.
Clarion	What was the cause? Explain it, pray.
Sigismund	I wanted to make love to a lady But those old bones appeared. I wanted to kill that old fool But the Cossack interfered.
Basilio	What, do you not respect a lady's honour? Don't you respect this good old man's grey hair?
Clotaldo	Her honour's untarnished. So is my grey hair.
Sigismund	I was brought up with horror and grey air. I'm getting ready for the day When I'll squash your Royal honour Under my boots and use your silver beard As a mat to wipe my feet on.
Basilio	Wild, monstrous, rash. O you are barbarous.

Sigismund   You brought me up like a rat in a box
                   But I'll be revenged on you, Grizzly-locks.

Basilio   Now I am sure the cruel stars spoke true.
                   All of you, mark him, mark his insolence.
                   You have all heard him. He would be revenged.
                   No, Sigismund my son, before that happens,
                   You'll sleep again where you slept yesterday.

                   [*The* KING *signals to the servants. They seize* SIGISMUND *and* CLARION.
                   The KING *pours a potion into* SIGISMUND's *mouth. He falls asleep.*]

Basilio   Now you shall think that everything which passed
                   Here in the palace on your happy day,
                   Like all good things on earth, was so much dreaming.
                   Clotaldo, take him back into the mountains.
                   Estrella and the Duke shall reign in Poland.

                   [*Exeunt. Enter* ASTOLFO *and* ESTRELLA]

Astolfo   I see, Estrella, that the stars spoke true:
                   Take Sigismund and myself, for we were born
                   Under two signs. For him there was foretold
                   A life of crime and it has come to pass;
                   But for my part, when I first saw your eyes
                   They were as stars, my stars, for then they spoke
                   To me of bliss and fame and great possessions.
                   Is it not so? Or are the fickle stars
                   True only when they tell of evil things?

Estrella   I do not doubt that these fine words of yours
                   Are finely meant, but are they meant for me?
                   What of the woman whose bewitching picture
                   You wore about your neck when we first met?
                   I think it must be so. These compliments
                   Belong to her, so go and take them to her,
                   And she'll reward you for your gentleness.
                   Kind words and courtesies to other women
                   Are scarcely current in the Court of Love

Astolfo   I never wear that portrait now. It chokes me.
                   I have made room for you and for your beauty.
                   For where Estrella is there are no shadows,
                   As there are no stars by the noonday sun.
                   I'll fetch the picture, madam.

                   [*Exit* ESTRELLA]

Fair Rosaura,
Forgive me now. I know too well that I
Do ill in this, but when a man or woman
Is separated from the one they love,
They rarely keep their faiths. And so with me.
I'll get the portrait.

[*Exit* ASTOLFO. *Re-enter* ESTRELLA]

Estrella
O how we act and do not show our minds.
I know he does not love me but he woos
In policy. And I in likewise act
And now seem cold. That's likewise policy,
For I believe that is the way to win him.

[*Enter* ROSAURA, *demurely dressed*]

Rosaura
[*Aside*] I changed my dress because I thought it safer.

Estrella
Astraea . . .

Rosaura
Yes, my lady?

Estrella
I am glad
That you have come. I have a secret for you.

Rosaura
You honour me and I obey you, madam.

Estrella
I have not known you long and yet I trust you.
I want to share my inmost mind with you.

Rosaura
I am your slave.

Estrella
Then as you know, Astolfo,
Who is my cousin, means to marry me,
Which it is hoped, will cancel much misfortune
With one great joy. But though I dote on him
I dare not show it. Something troubles me.
When he arrived in Poland he was wearing
A portrait of a lady round his neck.
I asked him if he loved her. He denied it.
He's gone to fetch it but I'd be embarrassed
To take it from him. You stay here instead,
And when he comes ask him to give it to you.

[*Exit* ESTRELLA]

Rosaura
What woman is there wise and calm enough
To know what she should do if she was I?
When I was man, I wished I was a woman,

But now I am I wish I was a man.
O what a pickle and a maze I'm in:
I curse the hour that I was born feminine.
I'm sworn to serve Estrella and to get
My picture back. I'm sworn to obey Clotaldo
Who saved my life. He said I must not woo
Astolfo, yet I'm sworn to or to kill him.
Nor am I now suited to please the man.
I fear that I am ugly, dull and nasty.
I am the fool of love. What shall I do?
I can't pretend, I. When Astolfo comes,
However much I plan and I prepare
I'll do . . . O God, I don't know what I'll do.

[*Enter* ASTOLFO]

Astolfo   Here is the portrait, madam . . .
Good God!

Rosaura   What troubles you?
Why do you stare at my face?

Astolfo   To see you in this place.
Rosaura . . .

Rosaura   I am sorry, sir,
You're very much mistaken,
I am called Astraea.
I'm a lady-in-waiting.
I am not the noble lady you seek,
If I may judge by the way you speak.

Astolfo   Do not pretend, Rosaura,
What if you're called Astraea,
I love you as Rosaura . . .

Rosaura   I do not understand one word you utter.
So please your highness, all that I can say
Is that Estrella (who may be the star
Of love itself, since that's Estrella's meaning)
Told me to wait for you and in her place
To take a picture which you'd bring for her.
The lady wants it and I must obey her.

Astolfo   Inform your eyes, they contradict your voice.
If you uttered lies with perfect control
I'd look through your eyes and see your soul.

Rosaura	I want the picture. That is why I'm here.
Astolfo	Then, if you want to lie like you do. Go to the princess and say this, Astraea: She asked me for a picture but I prize her Too much to send her such a petty gift, Instead of that, in love and in devotion, I send her now the sweet original. Go, take it to her. You are bound to take it Wherever you may go.
Rosaura	If I return With the original and not the copy I shall have failed my duty to my mistress. I came for the portrait. Give me the portrait. I must have the portrait.
Astolfo	I will not give it And you cannot take it.
Rosaura	I'll tear it from you. You devil. Let go.

[*She tries to seize it*]

Astolfo	What use is that?
Rosaura	By God, I will not let it fall Into another woman's hands.
Astolfo	You admit you're Rosaura. You said that you'd give it Back to your mistress.
Rosaura	I do not care what I said.
Astolfo	You're angry.
Rosaura	You're base.
Astolfo	That's enough. You are mine.
Rosaura	I am not, you lie. You bully, you liar.

[*She grabs the picture again. Enter* ESTRELLA]

Estrella	Astraea. Astolfo. What is this?

Astolfo	Estrella.
Rosaura	[*Aside*] Love, grant me all your cunning So I can get the picture. My lady, I'll explain.
Astolfo	Now what's her plan?
Rosaura	Madam, you told me to wait For Astolfo to bring a portrait. I was day-dreaming: You know the way. I remembered A portrait of my own. I opened it but dropped it. Then Astolfo came. He would not give me his But picked up mine instead And would not give it back. I pleaded but he held on, So I tried to take it from him. There it is, in his hand. It's mine. It looks like mine.
Estrella	Astolfo, give it to me.
Astolfo	Madam . . .
Estrella	It flatters you: There is a calm about it.
Rosaura	Yes, it's my portrait.
Estrella	I do not doubt it.
Rosaura	Then you should order him To give you the other one.
Estrella	Take your own and go.
Rosaura	[*Aside*] Now I've got mine back I'll watch and see what happens.
Astolfo	Madam, I can explain . . .
Estrella	Give me the picture which you promised me. Although I hope that I shall never see you Or speak to you again, I do not want it To stay in your hands. I see I was foolish To ask for it. So give it back again.
Astolfo	Lovely Estrella, I do not know how I can return the portrait.

Estrella	Do not try.

Flirt with my servant: so much for your love.
I don't want your picture. Whatever you do
It would only remind me I begged it of you.

[*Exit* ESTRELLA]

Astolfo Estrella listen!
Damn you Rosaura. Everything was fine
Till you arrived in Poland. You'll destroy me.
My hopes hang on this marriage. If it fails
I'll tear Rosaura's eyes out with my nails.

[ROSAURA *comes forward*]

Rosaura Then tear them out. I will be glad of it.

Astolfo Rosaura, you have done much mischief to me.

Rosaura Astolfo, you have done much mischief to me.

Astolfo That's past. What you've just done will undo Poland
You see how Sigismund's unfit to reign.

Rosaura You're not fit either. You have broke your oath.

Astolfo Yes, I did as the world does.

Rosaura   Then you're base
As mean men are.

Astolfo   I could not marry you
(I see that I must spell it out again)
Because you do not know who was your father.
You know that is our law, our code, our custom.
I will not, cannot go against my honour.

Rosaura You went against it when you mangled mine.

Astolfo It's true I did you wrong . . .

Rosaura   Why then,

Astolfo   No, listen.
You do wrong now to make so much of it.
Love does not last. It fades. To cling to it
When it is done is tedious and foolish.
I know that you love to torment yourself:
You hug your woes just as your mother did.
That's why you serve Estrella and that's why
You tried to get me to give up your picture.

Rosaura	You're full of reasons but what's in your heart? Tell me one thing.
Astolfo	What?
Rosaura	Do you love Estrella?
Astolfo	I will not tell you. If I said I did You'd plague yourself, and if I said I did not You'd go on clinging to your hopes and dreams.
Rosaura	To live in doubt's a plague.
Astolfo	That's how you are. You twist and turn all that I say to you. That is your woman's nature.
Rosaura	You are vile. You twist and turn, not I. That's your man's nature. You broke your oath but I will not break mine.
Astolfo	What have you sworn?
Rosaura	Either to marry you Or kill you. Why do you laugh?
Astolfo	You can do neither.
Rosaura	Let time tell that.
Astolfo	No, let time tell it now. I challenge you. Here is my dagger. Use it.
Rosaura	I will not kill you with a mean man's weapon. I am sworn to slay you with my father's sword.
Astolfo	Well, keep your oath.
Rosaura	I do not have it with me.
Astolfo	Fetch it and I will wait. Why, it's apparent You cannot do it. Now I know that I Did right when I forsook you, for I see You are not of noble blood. Do not reproach me That I'm forsworn, for you are now as I am. Therefore have done, go home to Muscovy, Forget what's past and get yourself a husband, And talk no more of vengeance, oaths and honour. [*Aside*] Some men might say that was quite a close call. But I know about love. There was no risk at all.

[*Exit* ASTOLFO]

Rosaura	Alas. I'm worse off than I was before.
	O what a fool I was. Alone with him:
	I should have wooed him or I should have killed him.
	All that he said is true. I have no honour.
	I am forsworn. I do torment myself.
	I am a mingle, I am full of voices
	That war in me and buzz inside my head.
	I cannot help it. I am as I am.
	It cannot be but that I have bad stars.
	What shall I do? How shall I find a clearness?
	An oath is clear, and I will keep mine yet.
	Then, stars, be kind and help me find a way
	To kill Astolfo. There's no more to say.

[*Exit* ROSAURA]

Scene 2

[CLOTALDO *and* GUARDS *carry in* SIGISMUND *and* CLARION. *They leave* SIGISMUND *on the floor and chain him.*]

Clotaldo	He has had his day.
1st Guard	Here's his old rusty chain.
Clotaldo	His pride has led him back
	Into black night again.

[*Exit* CLOTALDO *and* GUARDS]

Clarion	Somnolent, somniferous.
	When the arms of Morpheus
	Give you back to consciousness
	You will find your luck
	Has drowned in the black lake.
	All your pomp is muck:
	It was all a fake.
	Your life is a game,
	A little shadow-play
	Lit by death's candle-flame
	For one brief day.

[*Re-enter* CLOTALDO *with a candle*]

Clotaldo	You talk too much.
	Go, chain him in a cell.
Clarion	Why me?

Clotaldo	You know too much. You're a noisy Clarion.
Clarion	What have I done? I ask you? Have I ever tried To kill my father or something worse? Or tried to rape a Princess? Never! Quite the reverse. Do I throw servants in the lake? Do I get reborn, for God's sake? Do I dream? Do I sleep? I do not. So Why lock me up?
Clotaldo	Because of what you know.
Clarion	At least make sure I'm properly fed With plenty to drink.
Clotaldo	[*To* GUARDS] You heard what he said.

[GUARDS *take* CLARION *out. Enter* KING BASILIO, *cloaked and masked.*]

Basilio	Clotaldo.
Clotaldo	Sire, why have you come disguised?
Basilio	It was perhaps unwise but I am curious To see what happens now to Sigismund.
Clotaldo	Well, there he lies as he did formerly.
Basilio	Unlucky Prince. Tragic nativity.
Clotaldo	He's restless. He is talking in his sleep.
Basilio	What does he dream of now? We'll listen to him.
Sigismund	[*In his sleep*] Princes show mercy when they murder tyrants. I'll crush Clotaldo. He'll be old dead meat. Where is my father? Let him kiss my feet.
Clotaldo	He threatens me with death.
Basilio	And me with shame.
Sigismund	[*In his sleep*] I will be brave, my cue is blood and vengeance. I'll be revenged upon the King, my father, And trample him in dust on this great stage, The theatre of the world . . .

[*Wakes*]

O where am I?
Light . . . darkness . . . Fetters again?
A slave? What things I've dreamed of . . .

Clotaldo [*Aside*] I will delude the Prince.
Time to wake up. Have you slept all day long?
We talked last night of eagles, and I think
You've slept since then.

Sigismund I've slept since then . . .

Clotaldo I've tracked
An eagle in the air while you were sleeping.

Sigismund I think that I am still asleep, Clotaldo.
It must be so, for if the things I saw
When I was dreaming were so clear and bright,
What I see now must be unreal and shadows.

Clotaldo Tell me your dream.

Sigismund If it had been a dream
I would not tell it. What I saw, Clotaldo,
I saw indeed, and it was real I saw.
I woke. And then I saw myself, in bed
Soft comforting, the cover sweetly woven
Like spring time meadows in our mountain lands,
Cornflower, wild strawberry and lady's slipper.
Courtiers knelt and hailed me as their Prince,
And then you told me I was Prince of Poland.

Clotaldo And when I told you that, how did you thank me?

Sigismund Not well. I think I tried to kill you twice.
Yes, I was angry and I called you traitor.

Clotaldo Were you so cruel?

Sigismund I thought I saw my father
And hated him. For I was all men's master
And wanted my revenge upon them all,
Except one woman whom I know I loved.
The rest have vanished, but her picture is
Branded upon my mind. She must be real.

[*Exit the* KING]

Clotaldo   [*Aside*] The King has gone. He's moved.
                      Because we talked a while last night of eagles
                      You dreamed of empires when you went to bed.
                      But you would do well, even in your dreams,
                      To honour those who care for you each day.
                      Kindness is never wasted, even in dreams,
                      And gentleness is never thrown away.

                      [*Exit* CLOTALDO]

Sigismund   Perhaps that's true. Perhaps I should snuff out
                      This flame of rage, this blaze of red ambition.
                      The time may come when we shall dream again.
                      In this strange world to live's a kind of dreaming,
                      And each of us must dream the thing he is
                      Till he awakes. The King dreams he's a King,
                      Lives, orders, governs in a royal illusion,
                      Because his fame is written in the wind.
                      For every King that rules men in his King-dream
                      Must wake at last in the cold sleep of death.
                      The rich man dreams his riches which are cares,
                      The poor man dreams his penury and pain,
                      The man who prospers dreams, the man who strives,
                      The man who hurts men, and the man who's hurt,
                      All dream. So what's this life? A fraud, a frenzy,
                      A trick, a tale, a shadow, an illusion.
                      And all our life is nothing but a dream.
                      And what are dreams? They are no more than dreamstuff.
                      And what is real is nothing, and a man
                      Is nothing neither.

                      [*Snuffs out the candle*]
                                          It is all a dream.

                      [*Exit* SIGISMUND. *Enter* CLARION]

Act Three

Scene 1

Clarion	[*Sings*] Lord, I am a drinking man With nothing left to lose. My quest is for oblivion, My weapon is the booze. My enemy's reality - I dodge her when I can. God bless the drinking man . . . Lord, I am a drinking man. I'm drinking to forget Something I remembered When my memory was wet. O brandy sun, shine down on me And give me tippler's tan. God bless the drinking man . . . Though they've locked me in a cell Like Cervantes in the clink, I shall manage very well, If I have enough to drink. I'll swig it from a goblet, I'll sip it from a can, God bless the drinking man . . . Lord, I am a drinking man And when I die of thirst, Place me in a champagne vat, Totally immersed. An after-life of stupor Is my religious plan. God bless the drinking man . . . [*Drums. Clamour and banging outside. Enter* SOLDIERS]
1st Soldier	This is the tower. Where is the prisoner?
Clarion	It must be me that they are looking for.
2nd Soldier	He's here.
Clarion	No, he's not here.

1st Soldier	Your Majesty.
Clarion	You must be drunk.
1st Soldier	You are our rightful prince.
2nd Soldier	We want our natural lord.
3rd Soldier	No Muscovite.
2nd Soldier	No foreign prince for us. Break off his chains.

Clarion
It's real. They are not joking. They want me.
It must be a custom in this curious kingdom
To make someone a prince here for a day
And then to throw him back in jail again.
And now it's my turn.

3rd Soldier	We kiss your feet, sire.
1st Soldier	Sir, give us your feet.
Clarion	I can't. I need them. Princes need their feet.
2nd Soldier	What is your will, my lord?
Clarion	What is my will?

Now I am Prince of Poland
I'll free all drunks and debtors.
I'll put the politicians
Respectfully in fetters.

I promise to my subjects
Steaks shall grow on trees
And a cathedral shall be carved
From Gorgonzola cheese.

My kingdom's cows shall give us
Vodka instead of milk.
Harlots will pay their clients
And beggars sleep in silk.

My policy for Poland
Is: set the people free.
And when I say the people,
I mean people like me.

1st Soldier	We've told the King We want no other prince but you to rule us.
Clarion	Did you not treat my father with respect?
2nd Soldier	We spoke out of our loyalty to you.

Clarion	If you were being loyal then I forgive you.
1st Soldier	Prince Sigismund, come forth and rule your kingdom.
Clarion	That seems to be the name they give to all Their player princes.
Soldiers	Long live Sigismund.

[*Enter* SIGISMUND]

Sigismund	Who calls on Sigismund?
1st Soldier	Who is this man?
Clarion	That is the true prince. I am just a player. I abdicate.
1st Soldier	Which one of you is the prince?
Sigismund	I have been told that I am.
2nd Soldier	Little fool, Why did you say you were?
Clarion	I didn't, you did. You Sigismunded me. You are the fool, Not I.

[*Exit* CLARION]

1st Soldier   Enough of this. Prince Sigismund.
Your father is a clever, cunning man
But he believes the world's run by the stars.
He is afraid of prophecies which say
He will kneel at your feet. Therefore he wants
To lock you up, deprive you of your rights
And give them to the Duke of Muscovy.
And to that end he called a parliament
And so awoke the people. We know now
That we already have a native heir
And do not want a foreigner to rule us,
Especially a Muscovite. So come with us.
We all know how to fight. The mountain's swarming
With soldiers, outlaws, peasants, prisoners,
Who hail you as their King. Then come away
And seize the crown and sceptre from the tyrant.

[*Drums and trumpets*]

Soldiers	Long live King Sigismund.

Sigismund
It sounds again.
What do you want with me this time, you stars?
Another bubble? Another shadow-play?
And will it once more vanish in the dark?
No, not again. No dreaming. I'll not do it.
Ghosts, go away. You all seem to have bodies
And voices, but you have none. You are shadows.
You are like me: you are asleep. You're dream-men.
I will not be the plaything of the stars.
I will not be like some rash almond tree
Which buds too soon so that its pink and white
Shatters like glass in the first ruthless frost
And all its loveliness and light is lost.

1st Soldier
If you believe that we are lying to you,
Look at the mountainside: all those men are with us.

2nd Soldier
They await your orders.

Sigismund
Yes, I see them clearly.
I see you clearly too. But once before
I saw as clear as that but I was dreaming.

1st Soldier
My lord, they say before a great event
There's some great sign. Your king-dreaming was an omen
To make you ready.

2nd Soldier
This event is real.

Sigismund
What are your names?

1st Soldier
We don't have names, my lord.

2nd Soldier
We leave our names at home.

3rd Soldier
It's dangerous
To use real names.

Sigismund
How many of you are there?

1st Soldier
We're numberless.

2nd Soldier
As stars are.

3rd Soldier
You could say
That we go on forever.

Sigismund
I believe
You speak the truth and my dream was an omen.
Let us suppose that. But what then? Life's brief,
So let us dream. And yet I know my nature.
Therefore I must remember as I dream

I must be politic. Let's all remember
That we must wake up when we least expect it.
Since we know that and know that we must suffer
We'll suffer less because we know we shall.

Sigismund   I will go on. I thank your loyalty.
I'll free you all from foreign rule in Poland.
I'll prove the stars spoke true and make my father
Grovel before me . . . if I don't wake up . . .

Soldiers   King Sigismund!

[*Drums. Enter* CLOTALDO]

Clotaldo   Guards! Where are the guards?

Sigismund   It is Clotaldo.

Clotaldo   I kiss your feet. I know that I must die.

Sigismund   No. You must be the North Star in my sky.
Stand up, Clotaldo, do not be afraid.
You must still be my guide and counsellor.

Clotaldo   What do you mean?

Sigismund   I mean that I am dreaming.
But I would like to act well in my dream.

Clotaldo   If doing good is now your game
Do not be surprised
If I want to do the same.
You do not know these men.
If you'll wage war against your father
How can I be your adviser?
He is my King. All I can do
Is offer up my life to you.

Sigismund   I am your King. You are a traitor to me.

1st Soldier   Your fine words are a mockery, Clotaldo.

Clotaldo   You are all traitors. Where's your loyalty?

2nd Soldier   We are the loyal ones and you are the traitor.

Clotaldo   Rebellion is damnation in a subject.

3rd Soldier   To be a subject is the true damnation.

Clotaldo   You twist my words.

1st Soldier   You twist reality.

Sigismund   Enough of this.

Clotaldo	My lord . . .
Sigismund	Clotaldo, listen:

If that is how you feel, go to the King.
Don't try to tell me what is good or bad,
I think that each man's honour is his own.
Farewell. We'll meet in battle.

Clotaldo   You're generous, but if you hope to reign,
You must remember things may change again.

[*Exit* CLOTALDO]

Sigismund   Now to the Palace. Drums and trumpets, sound.

[*Drums and trumpets*]

Come Zodiac, we go to reign.
I am as my stars make me.
If this is real don't let me sleep.
If I'm asleep, don't wake me.
What matters is to try
To do what is right.
Then if it is real
Right justifies itself,
And if it is unreal
It does no harm to have
Some credit up in heaven.
It may be useful on the day
That we awake and end the play.

[*They go out of the prison*]

Scene 2

[*Enter* ESTRELLA *and* ROSAURA]

Estrella   He picked it up? You did not give it to him?

Rosaura   No, madam.

Estrella   Swear it, girl.

Rosaura   I swear I did not
Give him my picture, no, not yesterday.

Estrella   I'm satisfied. Forgive me my jealousy.

Rosaura   I understand it.

Estrella   Then you know it is
A monster that preys most where love is greatest.

Rosaura	I know.
Estrella	Then help me.
Rosaura	I will do your will.
Estrella	I am on fire. Astolfo treats me cruelly But I love him the more. I burn for him, I ache for him, Astraea. Yet I've sworn That I will never speak to him again. How may I then undo what I have said?
Rosaura	I think you cannot.
Estrella	No, I think I can. Because our marriage is a thing of state I've never spoken with the Duke in private. I long to do so and to know his nature To judge if he is fit to marry me.
Rosaura	Indeed?
Estrella	I have a bower in my garden That's walled around, a pleasant secret place. Give him this key and bid him enter in. Say I'll be there tonight but do not tell him I gave it to you but rather say you are His friend, not mine. Take it, Astraea. Take it.
Rosaura	And when he comes, what then?
Estrella	I do not know. Time must try that. Now I am wild with love And I must have my will. I long for night And for Astolfo. Heaven do me right.

[*Exit* ESTRELLA]

Rosaura	I'll get a copy of this garden key: Then when he comes, God knows who he will see.

[*Exit* ROSAURA. *Enter* KING BASILIO *and* ASTOLFO]

Basilio	But who can stop a bolting horse, Astolfo? Or stop a river roaring to the sea? Such is the pride and anger of the people: Some shout "Astolfo", others "Sigismund". My realm is turned into a stage for Fate To play out monstrous tragedies of blood.
Astolfo	I see I must forget my love awhile. Now war must serve. This is no time for wooing.

If Poland now resists me as her heir
It is because I have not proved myself,
And yet one day I'll sit upon her throne.
I'll take a horse. I'm proud and I am angry.
I'll strike those rebels like a thunderstone.

[*Exit* ASTOLFO]

Basilio   O it is dangerous, foreseeing danger.
I ran away and ran to what I ran from.
I hid a thing, and hiding it I found it,
And so I have destroyed my own dear land.

[*Enter* ESTRELLA]

Estrella   Your majesty, you must go now in person
And curb the turmoil raging in the streets,
For everything is havoc and confusion.
They clamour that you should release your son.

[*Enter* CLOTALDO]

Clotaldo   Thank God you're safe, sire.

Basilio   Where is Sigismund?

Clotaldo   The rebels found the tower and freed the Prince.

Basilio   Basil the Learned. What's my learning won?
Basil the Great. What has my greatness done?
This is the ruin of my lovely land.
The winds have died. The stars, the sun have gone.
The houses and the farms stand now like tombs.
Each soldier is a walking skeleton.
I see this nightmare with my eyes wide open;
Before me stands an enormous hill
Of men and horses, red and broken,
And the whole hill cries out and will not be still.

Clotaldo   There's some organ in man
That seems to need death
As the heart needs blood,
As the lungs need breath.

Estrella   What I would do
Cannot now be done.
And yet there's a battle
Still to be won.

Basilio   Yes, I'll ride out
To meet my son.

[*Exit* KING BASILIO *and* ESTRELLA]

Clotaldo	Why did he tell his son he was his father? That has bred chaos. That was his mistake. I'll never tell my daughter who I am For fear lest Fortune throws me in the lake.

[*Enter* ROSAURA *with her father's sword and a skull*]

Rosaura	The Duke must die.
Clotaldo	What would you now, Rosaura? What is this show? What is this skull of death?
Rosaura	It is myself. For when Astolfo left me I died. So he must die.
Clotaldo	No.
Rosaura	Hear me out. Tonight he meets Estrella in a garden. You told me that he woo'd in policy But now I see it's lust. Then take this key And this your sword and there cut down Astolfo. Uphold my honour. Give me my revenge.
Clotaldo	Skulls, garden keys . . . Why this is fantasy. The Duke has gone to fight Prince Sigismund.
Rosaura	Then you must follow him.
Clotaldo	I cannot do that.
Rosaura	You swore to help me And you must keep your oath.
Clotaldo	I did plan for your honour's sake To kill him if I could, A tumble into the lake Or a garotte in the wood. But then the young prince tried To crush me murderously And I surely would have died But Astolfo rescued me. I owe him my life, so how Can I kill him now? I'm bound to him and you: So what am I to do?
Rosaura	You are a man. You know the code.

Giving is noble
But receiving's base
You gave me life
So I ennoble you.
You received life from him
So you owe him nothing.
Do you accept that?

Clotaldo   Yes, in principle.
Yet though giving shows nobility
The generous must condemn
All those who react ungratefully
To those who succour them.
My reputation is unmarred
And I find meanness hateful.
My good name would be scarred
Were I to prove ungrateful.
I respect in my liberality
Giving and receiving equally.

Rosaura   You said to me that life
Without honour is no life,
So the life you gave me
Is no life at all.
And if being generous
Comes before being grateful
(As you seem to say),
I'm waiting for my life:
I haven't got it yet.

Clotaldo   You have convinced me.
But what can we do?
We must find you sanctuary.
I will give you all my wealth.
You shall live in a nunnery.
The advantages are three:
One, no civil feud;
Two, I deal generously;
Three, I show my gratitude.
There, I don't believe
I could hatch a better plot
If I was your father;
I'm sure I could not.

Rosaura   If you were my father
I'd take the insult:

	Since you're not, I will not. Money and a nunnery!
Clotaldo	Were I your father . . .
Rosaura	I would spit at you.
Clotaldo	You are forsworn Because you swore to kill him. Do not reproach me If I am forsworn too.
Rosaura	Then I'll kill the Duke myself.
Clotaldo	I don't believe you.
Rosaura	I swear I will do it.
Clotaldo	You are a woman And you have such courage?
Rosaura	Yes.
Clotaldo	What inspires you?
Rosaura	My good name.
Clotaldo	Astolfo Is going to be . . .
Rosaura	My honour.
Clotaldo	Both your King And your Estrella's husband.
Rosaura	I'll prevent him. By God, I swear it.
Clotaldo	This is madness.
Rosaura	Yes.
Clotaldo	Then stop it.
Rosaura	I cannot.
Clotaldo	Then you will lose . . .
Rosaura	I know I will.
Clotaldo	Your honour and your life.
Rosaura	I well believe it.
Clotaldo	What do you gain?
Rosaura	My death?

Clotaldo	This is mere spite.
Rosaura	It's honour.
Clotaldo	No, it's madness.
Rosaura	It's courage.
Clotaldo	No, it's frenzy.

Rosaura
                 No, it's rage:
I call it rage.

Clotaldo
         No, it is jealousy.
You're jealous of your mistress.

Rosaura
I do not care if it's jealousy
Or spite or rage or madness.
I have so many passions
I don't know which is greatest.
I will do it alone.

[*Exit* ROSAURA]

Clotaldo
Stars, show us all some shrewd way out of this,
If you know one. O there is such confusion.
Above the omens of the skies are bad.
Below, it's worse. I fear the whole world's mad.

[*Exit* CLOTALDO]

Scene 3

[*Trumpets and drums. Enter* SIGISMUND, *armed, with his soldiers.*]

Sigismund
I wish that Rome could see me here today,
Rome in her heyday, in her golden age.
Would not her legions laugh and whoop for joy
To see a wild beast marching at the head
Of such an army, great and proud enough
To conquer heaven? No, that's not the way
To mock illusion. Let's return to earth.
Before the gold sun sinks in the dark green sea
We will unthrone the King.

[*Enter* CLARION, *followed by* ROSAURA *on horseback*]

Clarion
Here comes a horse, a tumultuous steed
(Pardon me, but I feel the need
To make a vivid, poetical speech)
Its mouth foams round the bit like a sea-beach,

Its breath pounds like the hurricano,
Its heart pulses like a ripe volcano.
A horse of fire and water, earth and air:
Rosaura rides him. She is fair.

Rosaura   Honour: I wish to speak to you of honour.
Be generous, Sigismund. Your fame has sprung
From night's dim shadows into royal day,
And as the sun leaps from the arms of dawn
And bathes the hills and paints the shining sea-foam,
So may you now, that are the sun of Poland,
Shine upon me, a poor unhappy woman.
Three times we've met.
Three times you haven't known me.
First, I was a man
When you lay in prison
And your story eased me.
Second, I was a woman
When you were a King,
A dream King, a shadow.
Now I am whole,
I am both man and woman.
I had a love in Muscovy.
He is the Duke Astolfo.
He swore to marry me
But he broke his oath:
I seek revenge on him
As you seek it today
Against your royal father.

I wear both silk and steel.
Both of us wish to destroy this marriage.
I, that the man who is my lawful husband
May not be married to another woman;
You, to prevent Poland and Muscovy
Joining in one. Then as I am a woman,
Help me to win my honour. As I am man,
I say, go on and seize on Poland's crown;
Destroy Astolfo, do not let him have it.
Yet as I am woman, I beseech your pity
And pray you will be gentle now and kind.
Yet as I'm man, I offer you my sword.
But if you touch me as I am a woman,
Then as I am a living breathing man,
I will defend my honour like a man

And I will kill you. In this war of love
I am a woman in my woe and fury,
But as I am a man, I'm strong for honour.

Sigismund   What is the truth of this? I do not know.
If I have only dreamed my former greatness,
How can this woman speak of how she saw me?
Now counterfeits ring true and truth sounds hollow.
What does the shadow of a shadow look like?
What happens when two mirrors face each other?
If we cannot distinguish fact from fiction
Or what is real from what is an illusion,
Let's take the dream and use it to the limits
While we still can. Rosaura's in my power,
My heart shakes as her beauty shines on me.
What if she kneels? This is a dream. Enjoy it.
Regret it later. No, no. Work it out.
It is vainglory. All the good that's past
Is dreaming. We are born to disillusion.
Then if our pleasures are a little flame
Which the sharp wind will turn to ash and dust,
I'll hold to what is lasting and divine.
She tempts me but I'll turn from this temptation.
Sound the attack!

[*Alarum*]

Rosaura   Sir, look at me.
Look at me, my lord,
Doesn't my honesty
Deserve a single word?

Sigismund   I look away because it's necessary.
Rosaura, if I am to save your honour
I must be cruel both to you and me.
I will not answer you but I will act.
Don't look at me Rosaura, or my duty
Will be exterminated by your beauty.
I'll do you good if we thrive today
And save your honour. Soldiers, march away.

[*Drums. Exit* SIGISMUND *and* SOLDIERS]

Rosaura   What do these riddles mean? He's clear and strong
And will destroy a kingdom for revenge.
He is awake,
But I am . . . I am I.
[*Sings*]

Dreamed the world was simple
Sweet and gentle-eyed.
But when I woke up
There was a monster at my side.
Dreamed that I had thought of
A cunning clever scheme.
Then I began to laugh,
Like a clown in a dream.

[*Alarums. Enter* CLARION]

Clarion   With banners flowing and trumpets thrilling
The King is going to do some killing.

Rosaura   I'll throw myself with joy into this chaos.
I'll ride and fight beside Prince Sigismund,
The scandal and the wonder of the world.

[*Exit* ROSAURA. *Alarums*]

Clarion   Battle rages, let the hero
Hack his way into the middle.
I will play the role of Nero
At a distance on the fiddle.
If I want to feel compassion
I'll feel sorry for myself.
Watch the guns and sabres flashing,
Unmolested on my shelf.

[*Climbs up. Music continues*]

From up here I'll watch the show,
Safely from this perch of mine.
Death won't find me up here, so
I can give him the old sign.

[CLARION *hides above. Alarums. Enter* ASTOLFO]

Astolfo   A sword has cut my vein:
I bleed to death.
Is there nobody by
To bind my wound?
Is no one here among
These cruel rocks?
I faint. Help. Help me now.

[*Enter* ROSAURA *on horseback*]

Rosaura   My name is Death.

Astolfo   Lo, here's another furore.

Rosaura	I am your death.
Astolfo	Those are words, Rosaura.

I know you well from when we both were wooing:
You're good at talking but less good at doing.
You love to act but this is not a stage.
This blood is real. So is your father's sword.
Then keep your oath, Rosaura, if you can.

[*She unhorses and binds his wounds*]

I like you best when silent.

[*Alarums. Enter* BASILIO, ESTRELLA *and* CLOTALDO *in retreat*]

Basilio I need a new name. Basilio the broken-hearted.

Estrella The traitors triumph.

Clotaldo Your army has deserted.

Basilio All meanings change when a battle's done.
Traitors are patriots if they've won.

Estrella Now we must hide from your tyrannous son.

[*Shot within.* CLARION *falls wounded from his hiding-place*]

Clarion Heaven and Hell! I think I'm done.

Astolfo Who is this fellow?

Clotaldo Somebody's son.

Clarion Got any brandy? Hurts where I fell down.

Astolfo Who are you, man?

Clarion I'm just a bloody clown.
Hey! Can I give you
One bit of advice?
If you want to survive,
You ought to pick
The part where the battle
Is really thick,
Where the corpses pile up
In a rough pyramid.
It's a damn sight safer
Than hiding like I did.
You can't escape Fate,
The stars do not lie.
When God wants it

We have to die.
Hey friend, pass the cup.

[CLOTALDO *gives him a drink*]

Strange, it feels
Like I'm waking up.

[*Sings*]
A clown in a dream
Falling upside down
And when I woke up
I was a dream in a clown.

[*Dies*]

Basilio   When God wants it we have to die:
That truth is written in the sky.

Clotaldo   Yet it's not Christianity to state
There's no defence against men's fate.

[*Takes up* CLARION's *jacket and cap*]

Disguise yourself, and hide and wait.

Estrella   A horse is over here: he is swift and fleet.

Astolfo   Ride off. We'll cover your retreat.

Basilio   No, I'll await death in this place:
I want to look him in the face.

[*Alarum.* CLOTALDO *disguises the* KING *in* CLARION's *clothes*]

Astolfo   Take it and fly.

Clotaldo   And we will guard the way.

Estrella   Make haste my lord.

Astolfo   Escape while you still may.

[*Alarum. Enter* SOLDIERS. *They find the* KING's *robe*]

1st Soldier   The King's in hiding here.

2nd Soldier   Seek him out. And Astolfo,

1st Soldier   Search every cave and rock.

Clotaldo   O fly, my lord.

Basilio   Clotaldo, stand aside.

[*Enter* SIGISMUND, *horsed.* BASILIO *steps forward*]

Your hunt is over,
Prince, I am here.
Now make your carpet
Of my grizzled hair.
I am your prisoner.
Do what you must do:
Let the predictions
Of the stars come true.

Sigismund   [*To audience*]
You who have witnessed these high words and deeds,
Listen to me. Attend your lawful Prince.

[*He dismounts*]

Those star words, written by God
On the blue tablet of the sky,
Those books with diamond letters
Printed on sapphire pages,
They never cheat or lie.
The one who lies and cheats
Is the man who claims
He understands the stars.
My father to protect himself
Made me a beast-man.
I could have been gentle,
But raised in a monster's den
Of course I grew up
A monstrosity.

If it was prophesied that you would be
Killed by a beast, would it be sensible
For you to seek out sleeping beasts or beast-men
And wake them up? If you were warned, "The sword
You wear will be your death", would it be sense
To carry that same sword between your teeth?
If someone said, "A green and silver mass
Of salty water will be your sad grave",
Would it be sense to sail forth on the sea-waves
When they hurl up their curling, snow-topped peaks?
With all your wisdom this is what you did.

Look at this man. He tried to rule the stars
Yet now he kneels before me and is humble.
How can I quell the hate he's bred in me?
What shall I do? What is my way? My answer?
What's right for me to do at this brief moment?

My soul cries out for vengeance but I see
My victory must be my own surrender.
Sir, now that heaven has proved you wrong, I kneel
And offer you my neck to tread upon.

Basilio My son, my own son,
By this act I am reborn inside you.
You have overcome yourself.
You have overcome the stars.
You have won yourself a crown.

[BASILIO *crowns and robes* SIGISMUND. *Drums and trumpets*]

All King Sigismund.

Sigismund Then all of you mark well
How I mean to rule in Poland.
Since I would be a conqueror
I see that I must first
Make a conquest of myself.
Astolfo, you have a debt
To pay from long ago.
Take Rosaura by the hand
And pay the debt you owe.

Astolfo It's true there's a debt and obligation,
But think: she does not even know her name.
It would be base to wed . . .

Clotaldo   No, say no more.
Rosaura is as noble as yourself:
She is my daughter.
You loved me well girl, when you were my niece;
Then will you hate me now I am your father?

Rosaura I cannot tell.

Astolfo What, is this true?

Clotaldo   I did not wish it known
Until I saw her honourably married.
She is my daughter.

Astolfo   Then since this is so,
And I have no hope to rule in Poland
I'll keep my word. Give me your hand, Rosaura,
We're both forsworn.

Sigismund [*To* ROSAURA]
                              Come, take what you have dreamed of.

Clotaldo, you were loyal both to me
And to my father. Ask me anything
And I will grant it you.

Clotaldo   Then ask my daughter
To forgive me.

Sigismund   So I do. Embrace your father.
Now for Estrella. She must not be left
Unhappy by the loss of such a prince.
Lady, I'll find you out another husband
Who is, I think, as good in birth and fortune.
Give me your hand. You shall be Poland's Queen.

Estrella   I am content. It is good policy,
And so I trust I may in time be happy.

1st Soldier   What about us? Clotaldo fought against you
And yet you honour him. We made you King,
Rescued you from the tower and fought beside you:
What's our reward?

Sigismund   The tower. Chains. No daylight.
There is no need of traitors
When the work of treason's done.

Astolfo   How changed he is.

Rosaura   How wise.

Basilio   How like a king.

Sigismund   Do I surprise you? Do not be amazed.
Is it a wonder if a dream has taught me
A little wisdom, I should fear to wake
And find myself once more a prisoner?

[*To audience*]

Yet even if that time never arrives,
I believe now that all human lives
Are just like dreams. They come, they go.
Perfection is impossible, we know.
Then noble hearts, show mercy, thus,
And for our worst faults, gently pardon us.
Remember as you each pass on your way,
Our actors, our musicians and our play.

The Great Theatre
of the World

Characters
The Director
The World
King
Beauty
Rich Man
Peasant
Beggar
Child
Voice

The Music
All the lyrics are written to tunes on Side One of the Hesperion tape of Spanish music from 1547–1616. I have lettered these tunes from A to V and refer to them in that way, since I don't know the titles.

The Cast
The Child may be represented by a naked doll, but it should be beautiful, carved from wood and painted. If this device is used, the World should speak the lines of the Child.

This version of *The Great Theatre of the World* was commissioned by The Mediaeval Players and was toured by them from Autumn 1984 to Spring 1985 with the following cast:
Elizabeth Downes, Mark Heap, Martin Pople, Mark Saban,
Bridget Thornborrow and Roy Weskin.

Musicians: Susan Addison, David Allen, Michael Harrison, Stephen Jones, Simon Mansfield, Martin Page.

Administrator	Judith Clough
Costume Designer	Cath Fitzgerald
Assistant Musical Director	Giles Lewin
Company Stage Manager	Neil Marcus
Set Designer	Bettina Munzer
Assistant Director	Laurence Sach
Musical Director	Andrew Watts
Artistic Director	Carl Heap
Producer	Dick McCaw

Part One

The Company	[*Sing*] Saints and sinners, hear our song!

Rogues and angels, none must stay.
All and sundry, come along
To the universal play.
For the great theatre
For the great theatre
Yes the great theatre of the world
Is opening today.

Gentlefolk of every age
Leave your labour, come away.
See yourself upon the stage
In a most amazing play.
For the great theatre
For the great theatre
Yes the great theatre of the world
Is opening today.

[*Enter the* DIRECTOR, *with a starry gown and nine rays on his hat*]

Director

My little planet, my lovely planet,
I made you with these two hands.
My darling planet, my darkling planet,
You steal your light and heat from my heavens.

Your millions on millions of beautiful flowers
Reflect my millions of stars,
But their glowing, petalled galaxies
Are rooted in earth, and drink from the earth
And return to the earth when they fade into death.

My blue and green planet, my favourite planet,
You're a battlefield where earth, fire, air and water clash,
Where mountains, thunderbolts, oceans and hurricanes
Fight it out; where the albatross
Like a white ship struggles to ride your winds;
Squadrons of salmon soar in your rivers and seas;
Volcanoes explode and splash their scarlet
All over the black paint of the night;
People and animals stride freely on your mountains.

My ever-changing planet, my happy planet,
You are my whirling, my wonderful one,

Today, for all time, I will give you a name.
I have decided to call you – The World.

[*The* WORLD *appears*]

World   Who's calling me?
Who woke me up?
Who drags me out of my warm bedroom
Down in the centre of the globe?
Who pulls me out of myself?
Who's calling me?

Director   Your Director is calling you.
Your all-powerful Director.
I whisper – and your forests dance.
I raise my hand – your hills take shape.

World   Well, what do you plan to do?
Is there anything I can do for you?

Director   World, I am your Director.
You shall be my Stage Manager.
I've had a marvellous idea for a show
Which you shall stage so cleverly
That the whole Universe will applaud.

World   Well, I'll certainly do my best.

Director   I want you to make a festival
To celebrate my power
So when my greatness is made manifest
All Nature will rejoice.
Everyone loves it when a show really works
And the audience shouts "Bravo!"
Human life is nothing but acting, so
Let Heaven sit in the best seats
To watch a play on your stage, World.

As I'm Director and the play is mine,
It shall be acted by my company
Whether they want to act or not.
As I chose human beings to be
The most important creatures of all
They'll be the members of my company
And they shall act out, as well as they can,
The story of the play that's called The World.
I shall cast each in a suitable role.

Now an entertainment of this kind
Needs beautiful props and transformations
And richly-decorated costumes.
So now I want you, cheerfully,
To create all these and to make some sets
Which will stagger the chilliest audience.
Work quick as light, for I'm Director,
You are stage manager, humans the actors.

World   Great Director, the actors and I
Will obey your every word.
I am the Great Theatre of the World
And I am your Stage Manager
Here to carry out your orders,
For though the scenery is mine, the play is yours.
I'm here so each actor may act on me
And provide what each scene requires.

First I will draw a black curtain across
To represent the turmoil of Chaos,
For it is best to hide away
Our set till we begin the play.
And then the mists shall disappear
And putting the vapours of darkness to flight,
Two lights shall shine out, bright and clear,
For there's no entertainment without light.
One is the golden lamp of day,
The other is that diamond
Upon the forehead of the night
Which casts a subtle silver ray.

The first act shown upon our stage
Shall represent a simple age
When Nature ruled life's gentle dawn.
And then, about the time that Time is born
A shining garden shall be shown
With burning colours and sweeping line –
Prodigies of natural design.

Branchfuls of blossoms, pink in the pink light,
Will open up, amazed by their first sight
Of the sun climbing up the sky.
The trees will yawn and stretch their roots
And they shall bear delicious fruits
Unpoisoned as yet by the serpent's lie.
A hundred crystal streams shall travel gaily

Over a thousand pebbles and flow on,
Meandering among the fields where, daily,
A million pearls sing in the Dawn.
Rolling meadows shall make this place
A heaven for the human race.
If hills and valleys are needed, you decide –
Hills and valleys shall be supplied.
The earth shall open up giant furrows,
I'll lay down rivers in all these sections
Which, like rabbits chased out of burrows,
Shall scoot off in all directions.

That was all Act One Scene One, but
As yet no building, house or hut
Has been observed upon the earth. But you
Wait for this – Act One Scene Two!
Flash! And I summon up cities and ports,
Palaces, temples, farms and forts.
And when the earth cries out for rest
From the weight of all this stone on her breast,
The entire stage I shall transform
To one almighty thunderstorm,
With avalanches of foaming mud,
Whirlwinds of hail and a great flood.

Then, through that pandemonium,
A curved ship with a roof shall come,
Lost on the trackless waters so
It trembles, not knowing where to go.
But safely down in its wooden womb,
Humans and animals shall find room.
And the sign of peace shall leap across the sky –
Red, orange, yellow, green and blue,
Indigo and violet shall shine through,
Ordering the army of the waves to dry.
And the great earth itself shall shake
Like a dog when it steps out of a lake.

The Law of Nature we call Act One
And now its distance has been run.
Director, let Act Two commence,
It's called the Law of the Commandments.
This act, as well as an excellent text,
Shall have spectacular effects,
For I shall unbutton the Red Sea's waves
And out of Egypt, her former slaves,

The Israelites, shall bravely tramp
Nor ever get their sandals damp.
Not only that, but every night
A pillar of fire I shall light.
Each day a cloud-pillar shall cross the sand
To lead them towards their Promised Land.

Moses in a swift cloud shall fly
To collect the Law from Mount Sinai.
And the second act shall be done
With a fierce eclipse of the sun
When the sun shall turn blood-red
And then go black and appear to be dead
And the skies shall be shattered, the mountains rumble,
The woods shall wither and the cities crumble
And after this frenzied act shall pass
There'll be nothing left but ruins and the grass.

Now the third act shall take place.
Act Three, which we call The Law of Grace.
The last act is the greatest one
And many miracles shall be done.

Act One: The Law of Nature.
Act Two: The Law of the Commandments.
Act Three: The Law of Grace.

And then we come to the end of the play
And the World will burn both night and day
So that, from a million miles away
The earth shall look like one flame, one pure ray.
I'm sorry, but when I think of that day,
My tongue dries up, what I feel I can't say.
My body shudders when I think of it.
My mind shakes when I imagine it.
I am astonished I can even say it . . .
I feel myself burning when I picture it.
Oh let this scene of pain and rage
Be postponed to some far distant age
And then postponed again, so people may
Never see their planet burned away!

Three acts, and wonders shall be done
And I promise you, not one
Shall fail through any carelessness of mine –
And I'll make sure the actors are on time . . .
The stage is ready now, and without doubt

You have the wardrobe all worked out,
For unborn folk assemble in your mind
And there they have their parts assigned.

Exits and entrances? There's two –
Cradle and Grave – I think they'll do.
Costumes and props? All written down.
For the King – robes and a crown.
For the fine lady – dangerous good looks.
For the minister – schools and books.
For the Captain – courage and a sword.
For the nobleman – the title, Lord.
Scourges for monks, for thieves – bad deeds.
For the peasant – tools and seeds,
(Because of that fool Adam's disgrace
The peasant must work till he's red in the face).
The ordinary folk? Well, let them do
Whatever they find they are free to do.
Only the poor I will not dress
For their correct uniform is nakedness.

All of this preparation stops
Complaints that lack of certain props
Or the appropriate hat or garments
Hampered some actor in his performance.
Anyone who acts inefficiently
Can put the blame upon themselves, not me.
So come on humans, get yourselves dressed,
My great theatre shall be your test!

[*Exit* WORLD]

Director   Mortals, I shall call you though you've not been born,
For before you are born you live in my brain.
Although you cannot hear my voice,
Come to this green garden place
Where, among cedars and palms
I wait for you, to give you your parts.

[*Enter the* RICH MAN, *the* KING, *the* PEASANT, *the* BEGGAR, BEAUTY *and the*
CHILD]

King   Director, we are here in your control.
We have neither life, reason nor soul.
We're the dust at your feet and that's a fact.
Breathe on this dust so that we may act.

Beauty
We are only an idea of yours,
Neither life nor breath are ours.
We cannot feel cold or touch wood.
We do not know either bad nor good.
But if we're on our way to the world to act
You can give us our roles and that's a fact.
And then, whatever character we've got,
What can we do but accept our lot?

Peasant
Greatest Director, I'm at your command.
You created me with your hand.
You know how well I can act and sing –
You must do, for you know everything.
If my performance turns out limp or lame,
I'll be the only one to blame.

Director
I always knew that if all had a say
In which particular role they'd play
None would choose sadness or suffering –
Everybody would want to play the King.
The King's part – I can see the great attraction,
But it's an acting part, not real action.
Still I am Director and it is true
That I know which part suits each one of you.
Now I will cast you. You take the King's part.

[DIRECTOR *presents each with a scroll of paper as their parts are named*]

King
Sir, I thank you with all my heart.

Director
You play the part of Beauty in this play.

Beauty
Thank you. This is my lucky day!

Director
You play the Rich Man, full of power.

Rich Man
I too was born in a lucky hour.

Director
You there, you must play the Peasant.

Peasant
Is that a job? Or is it pleasant?

Director
Hard work, long hours and miserably paid.

Peasant
I won't be much good at that, I'm afraid.
Though Adam was my father, Lord, I ask
Please grant me a different, easier task.
I am ambitious and I've no doubt
I'd make a marvellous rich layabout.
I don't know this part, I'm hopeless with ploughs,

I hate shifting muck and I'm scared of cows.
If it was worth saying "Leave me out"
I'd say it, but I haven't much doubt
That "Leave me out" would be thought rude
By a director of your magnitude.
I'll be the lousiest actor of the lot.
For natural gifts, all I seem to have got
Are a thick skin and the sense to keep
My thoughts to myself when they run too deep.
I ask for wool and you send me snow.
But they say you are fair, that's just how things go,
So I won't grumble, I'll simply try to live.
And since you love me, will you please forgive
A little slowness in my part today?
I don't want to finish before the play.

Director   You play the Beggar, in raw poverty.

Beggar   Is that the role you give to me?

Child   What will I be when it comes to my turn?

Director   You'll be still-born.

Child   Then there won't be much to learn.

Director   I know all creatures, and I must
Find them all parts – the owl in her nest,
The lion in his cave know I am just –
Each receives the part that suits it best.

Beggar   This Beggar part, well I realise
That it seems right and proper in your eyes,
But if you didn't mind, sir, on the whole,
I'd rather swap it for another role.
All right, Lord, since I have to play
The beggar, there's one more thing to say.
Why, Lord, did it have to be me?
For the others this play's a comedy
But for me it's a bloody tragedy.
When you handed me my scroll
Didn't you also give me a soul
Equal to his who plays the King
And equal emotions? So what's the thing
Makes us so different? Not our blood.
If you'd moulded us out of different kinds of mud
So I had a more stolid temperament,
Less alive than his, I'd know what you meant.

Lord, you must have something else in mind,
And forgive me, but it does seem unkind
That the King takes a far better role
But he doesn't have a better soul.

Director   If you play the beggar with all your heart
It will please me as much as the King's part.
And when the play is over there will be
Between the two of you, equality.
Play your part well and I promise you this –
Your reward shall be equal to his.
You'll go howling hungry and covered with sores –
But the King's part is no better than yours.
For, under the Law which I have laid,
You are judged by how well your part is played
And what you have earned will then be paid.
After the play, your Director Lord
Will grant all the actors their reward
And the best of the actors shall see my face
And dine with me at my table of Grace.
And at that banquet there shall be
Among you a golden equality.

Beauty   What's the play's title, sir? I'd like to know.

Director   Do Good, for God Is God, is the name of the show.

King   It's most important that we should make
In such a significant piece, no mistake.

Rich Man   It's essential we be rehearsed.
I insist we rehearse it first.

Beauty   That's a good idea, but there's not much room.
How can you rehearse in the womb?

Beggar   Go on unrehearsed? You're off your head.

Peasant   I'd like to second what the Beggar said.
Her opinion is one I share –
Peasant and Beggar make a pretty pair.
Even those classic plays, which they revive
Ad nauseam, don't come alive
Without rehearsal. So how can we,
An unrehearsed, green company,
Hope to perform a new play properly?

Director   There's only one performance
So it must not be fudged.

I shall watch that performance
And on it you'll be judged.

Beauty   But how are we supposed to know
When to come on, and when to go?

Director   You won't know that before you start.
Just be prepared to begin your part.
Whether or not you receive acclaim
When your role is over, I'll call your name.

Beggar   I get stage fright. What if, on the day,
I can't think what lines I ought to say?

Director   I've thought about that, and, just in case,
The World, with the script of the Law of Grace,
Shall act as Prompter to assist
If an important line is missed
By King or Beggar and to show the way
When actors seem lost in the play.
The Law says exactly what you must do
So I hope there'll be no more complaints from you.
From now on each of you has Free Will.
The stage is ready. The audience is still.
Concentrate now. Take a deep breath.
Good luck on your way from birth to death.

                   [*Exit* DIRECTOR]

King   What are we waiting for? Let's go on!

All   Do Good, for God is God. We are born.

Saints and sinners, hear our song!
Rogues and angels, none must stay.
All and sundry, come along
To the universal play.
For the great theatre
For the great theatre
Yes the great theatre of the world
Is opening today.

Gentlefolk of every age
Leave your labour, come away.
See yourself upon the stage
In a most amazing play.
For the great theatre
For the great theatre
Yes the great theatre of the world
Is opening today.

[*As they are about to exit, the* WORLD *enters and stops them*]

World   Costumes and props are all in place
              For this brief play of the human race.

King   Robes and crown, please.

World   Why robes and crown?

King   They're in my part. Look, there, written down.

[KING *shows his scroll to* WORLD, *takes robes and crown and exits*]

World   Now the King's ready.

Beauty   Give me the colours of magnolia and jasmine.
              Give me the colours of rose and orange blossom,
              Hyacinth, cornflower and carnation,
              The flowers of Maytime in shining competition.
              Let the sun stare at my redness and whiteness.
              Let the sun be my sunflower, turning to my brightness.

World   Don't be so vain. Acting's a humble art.

Beauty   I'm only trying to live the part
              Of Earthly Beauty.

World   In that case
              Let snow and scarlet tint your face
              And crystals sprinkle rays of light
              To keep your beauty always bright.

[*The* WORLD *gives* BEAUTY *a posy of flowers*]

Beauty   Flowers form a carpet when Beauty passes
              And streams provide her with looking-glasses.

[*Exit* BEAUTY]

Rich Man Give me money, good luck and happiness.
              I have come to the world to be prosperous.

World   I'll tear my entrails out for you, Rich Man.
              Out of my bosom I'll rip every gem,
              Silver and gold, you shall have both of them,
              Treasures I hid away when Time began.

[*The* WORLD *gives the* RICH MAN *jewels*]

Rich Man Pride is a jewelled garment which
              Looks wrong on the poor – but it suits the rich.

[*Exit* RICH MAN]

World	Don't you want to ask, before you go For anything to help you in this show?
Child	I don't need anything, do I? Before I'm born I have to die. I'm in the world long enough to run From a warm dungeon to a freezing one.

[*Exit* CHILD – *or doll is put away by the* WORLD]

World	What do you need?
Peasant	Just what I've got.
World	Show me your script.
Peasant	I'd rather not.
World	You have the look and smell of the land. Are you to work as a farmhand?
Peasant	That's how he cast me. I couldn't say no. But I'd like to say –
World	– You'll be needing this hoe.

[WORLD *gives* PEASANT *a hoe*]

Peasant	This is an heirloom left me by Adam Whose life was ruined by his madam, For she wheedled him – suck it and see – And he bit a bit off the fruit from the tree. Bad acting that, by our begetter. Still, I don't suppose I'll do any better.

[*Exit* PEASANT]

Beggar	I've watched you handing out happiness But now the game has come round to me. I don't ask for an embroidered dress But the rags and patches of misery.
World	What is your part?
Beggar	My part is pain – Loneliness, sickness, filth, disdain, Having to beg, never able to give, Pestering people for the right to live, Hated by summer, by winter cursed, Torn by the hounds of hunger and thirst – All these I shall enact wholeheartedly For they're essential to true poverty.

World	I will give you nothing at all.
Beggar	No more?
World	That's all the world ever gives the poor.
	In fact I'm afraid I must take this dress
	For the poor must suffer from nakedness.

[*The* WORLD *takes a dress off the* BEGGAR]

Beggar	So some receive robes and precious stones
	While others are stripped down to the bare bones?
World	Some sing hooray, some sigh alas,
	These characters, each from a different class.
	A King, whose empire spans the earth.
	A Beauty who strikes the observer blind.
	A Rich Man swelling with wine and mirth.
	A Beggarwoman with an angry mind.
	A Child whose life simply starts and stops
	And a Peasant who works every hour of the day.
	These are the characters in our play
	And I have to supply them with costumes and props.
	Come and see the festivities they will make,
	Lord and Director, for your sake!
Director	Since I have planned this entertaining show
	To reveal my greatness to all below,
	I'll sit and watch whatever's done
	From my golden throne inside the sun.
	All you who enter the earth through a cradle
	And leave it via a grave,
	Your Director is looking down today
	To see how his actors behave.
World	[*Sings to Tune A*]
	Sun and Moon,
	Silver Stars
	Praise him.
	Let the birds and beasts
	Of sea and sky
	Praise the Lord,
	Let them praise the Lord.
Director	My favourite hymn, which Daniel did compose
	To give Nebuchadnezzar some repose.
World	Let me perform the prologue to this piece.
	It is as short as a lamb's fleece,

But it will mean that many souls are won.
[*Sings*]
Do Good, for God is God!
[*Speaks*]
My prologue's done.
Now I'm the Prompter. Oh! The play's begun.

Beauty

[*Sings to Tune J*]
Walk with me through the fields,
The fields of Maytime,
And see the smiling sun,
My admirer.
Walk with me through the fields,
Enjoy the Maytime,
The little flowers that shine for me,
And my songbirds singing,
And my songbirds singing.

Beggar

[*Sings, also to Tune J*]
I'm hungry,
Hungry,
Hungry now –
I hate them all.

Beauty

[*Sings to Tune J*]
Why must you be so harsh?
Enjoy this planet.
God made the world for us,
So enjoy it.
Why are there silks and fur?
So we can touch them.
Why is there fruit and meat and wine?
So we may enjoy them.

Beggar

[*Sings to Tune J*]
I'm hungry,
Hungry
Hungry,
Hungry now –
I hate you all.

Beauty

[*Speaks*]
I am Beauty
And my duty
Is to see and be seen.

Beggar

[*Speaks*]
I'm the Beggar

And I stagger,
Unloved and unclean.

[*The* BEGGAR *and* BEAUTY *part*]

World   They'll never live amicably –
Loveliness and Poverty.

Beauty   Let my hair spread out like a fishing net
And I'll catch a shoal of young hearts yet.

World   She doesn't know her part too well.

Beggar   What shall I cry through the streets of Hell?

Beauty   Where shall I sell my beauty most dear?

World   [*Sings*]
Do good, for God is God.
[*Speaks*]
                          She does not hear.

Rich Man   [*Sings to Tune K*]
I have money, I have power,
Let me use them for delight.
Let sweet music fill my hall,
Feast and dance both day and night.
Let my tables flow with wine,
Cook me game of every breed
And let Venus share my bed
And my heart grow great with greed.

[*Enter* PEASANT]

Peasant   [*Sings to Tune N*]
Nobody ever had such work as mine!
I break the breast of my mother planet.
I plough her brown face with wrinkles.
That's how I repay my mother's kindness.
Sickle and hoe are my sword and spear,
Fighting in cornfields and in the vineyards.
Springtime comes around and my fields are flooded,
Then summer comes and my crops are scorching.
All that's left over they take in taxes,
So don't complain if I raise my prices.
[*Slow*]
        No, I can't take less.
        No, I can't afford to.
        You can call it unfair,
        You can say what you like

But I work bloody hard.
The rain!
I'll make a fortune
If springtime's dry this year.
[*Fast*]
Then there'll be crowds round my stall at market.
I'll raise my prices, they'll have to pay me.
I'll buy a farm with a house and orchard,
There every evening I'll crack a bottle,
Supping my wine with my wife and children,
Watching the swifts at their acrobatics.
[*Slow*]
    But until that time
    What should I be doing?

World	[*Sings*] Do Good, for God is God.
Peasant	Sorry, I didn't catch that. Deaf as a post.
World	Give up your sin.
Peasant	When I give up the ghost.

[*Enter* BEGGAR]

Beggar	Wretchedness racks my body and mind. The earth is the best bed I can find. Although the sky's a fine blue canopy I'm frozen and fried alternately. Hunger tears at me like a knife. Lord, give me the strength to carry this life.
Rich Man	What shall I wear to display my riches?
Beggar	I can't even afford to scratch where it itches.
World	[*Sings*] Do Good, for God is God.
Beggar	That voice again! That consoling Law!
Rich Man	That voice again! What a fearful bore!
Beggar	It softens my heart.
Rich Man	It makes mine harden.
Beggar	Here comes the King to walk in his garden.
Rich Man	I am a rich man, and a rich man's son. I loathe bowing down to anyone.
Beauty	I'll stand by his path and arrange my dress So he'll be ensnared by my loveliness.

Peasant	I'll stand behind you. If the King sees me He'll slap another tax on the peasantry.
King	My empire's a pyramid of stones And I'm the topmost one. I am the absolute ruler Of all states beneath the sun. All the world bows down to me – What more is to be done?
World	[*Sings*] Do Good, for God is God.

Beggar	[*Sings to Tune U*]
	Through my wretched eyes I see them –
	Other People being happy.
	See the King enjoy his kingdom –
	    But he ignores me.
	See the Beauty with her mirror –
	    But she ignores me.
	And the rich
	Eat too much,
	Eat everything.
	Yes the rich
	Take too much,
	Take everything.

	See the peasant, he's exhausted, But he eats well. They all ignore me, But I'll approach them And beg.
	[*Speaks*] Beauty, hunger is eating me. For Christ's sake, give me charity.
Beauty	My darling mirror, can you suggest Which curls and ribbons suit me best?
Beggar	Am I invisible?
World	She doesn't feel For herself, let alone you, imbecile.
Beggar	Since you have riches and to spare, Could you let me have a small share?
Rich Man	Are there no doors for you to knock? You sprang out on me. Gave me quite a shock. You should wait outside like a farmyard cat Instead of barging in like that.

Beggar	Sir, don't be so hard on me.
Rich Man	Get out of here immediately.
Beggar	You squander so much on pleasure, so Won't you give me anything at all sir?
Rich Man	No!
World	The parable remains with us Of Dives and of Lazarus.
Beggar	My need is an outlaw, maddened thing, I even dare beg from the King. Can you spare me something, sir?
King	You must apply to my Chief Almoner.
World	You'll find a King always refers His conscience to his ministers.
Beggar	Peasant, God blesses you I know By multiplying each grain you sow. Please give me something to help me now.
Peasant	God multiplies the grain – I have to plough, And sow and reap and mow and sweat. Aren't you ashamed of begging yet? You've got two legs, two hands and a head – Get a job and earn your bread. Take this hoe, nip down the road – The farmer'll pay for what you've hoed.
Beggar	In today's play, which I don't find too pleasant, I'm cast as the Beggar, not the Peasant.
Peasant	But our Director would allow You to sweat a little behind a plough?
Beggar	Brother, you are hard on me.
Peasant	Sister, I've learned that I have to be.
Beggar	Nothing?
Peasant	All right. Finish this ale. And take this loaf. It's not too stale.

[PEASANT *gives* BEGGAR *a mug and a loaf*]

Beggar	You're well acquainted with poverty. That's why you alone help me. [*Staggers*] I'm fainting.

| King | I come to support her. |

| World | You must. Only you can help this daughter. |

[KING *catches the* BEGGAR *and helps her to her feet*]

| Director | I could correct their errors easily
But I gave Free Will to humanity
Because I wanted them to have the chance
Of triumphing over circumstance.
That's why I let them play so freely here
And through their chaos, the Law of Grace says clear: |

| World | [*Sings*] Do Good, for God is God.
[*Speaks*] I warned them all together and one at a time,
It'll be their own fault if they commit a crime.
Now love your neighbour as yourself and –
[*Sings*] Do good, for God is God. |

| King | Since our lifetime is a pilgrimage
And we all travel in one company,
Let us converse convivially
Before the time when we must quit the stage. |

| Beauty | Without conversation, there's no life. |

| Rich Man | Let's each tell a story. A rich man and his wife – |

| Peasant | That'd take too long. |

| King | So what shall we do? |

| Beauty | Let us try to say what we think is true. |

| King | [*Sings to tune B*]
See my empire spread around the whole world,
See my majesty and glory.
I have palaces and gardens,
I have fortresses and armies.
I have beauty as a servant of mine.
I rule savages and nobles too.
Let me rule this mighty empire [*Back to line 2 of tune*]
Rule this many-headed monster.
Let me rule the monster wisely.
Let me rule the monster wisely. |

| World | [*Speaks*] Solomon asked for wisdom, too. |

| Voice | [*Sings to Tune B*]
Monarch of this fleeting empire,
Leave behind your vain ambitions,
For the part you played is over. |

King   [*Speaks*] A sad voice sings that my part's over.
                 My mind won't work. My tongue won't move.
                 I've finished my part. I want to exit.
                 But where shall I go?
                 I can't go backwards, no I can't go backwards
                 To the first door where my cradle stood.
                 Oh, this is hard.
                 I can't take one small step towards the cradle –
                 Each footstep takes me closer to the grave.
                 The water may lie in a garden pool,
                 Then spring up in a fountain into the light,
                 Shine in a thousand diamond drops,
                 And then, poor water, fall back to the pool.
                 Man, who was made from clay,
                 Must go back to the clay.
                 And never be himself again.
                 Supreme Director, since my time is spent,
                 Forgive my sins, for I repent.

                 [*Exit* KING *through the grave door, which all of them have to go
                 through*]

World   He ends his part impressively.

Beauty   He left behind his honour and fine company.

Peasant   I'll tell you this, if we've got no King
                 We'll be better off – if it rains next spring.

Beggar   It's a shame to die.

Beauty   Confusing too.
                 Without him, what are we going to do?

Rich Man   We can carry on our conversation without him.
                 What are you thinking about?

Beauty   Not about him!

World   How soon the survivors are consoled!

Peasant   Especially those he left land and gold.

Beauty   [*Sings to Tune E*]
                 I can see my loveliness.
                 I don't envy Kings their conquests
                 For my beauty conquers men
                 And they form my living empire.

                 Kings may win control of lives
                 But I wear hearts like a necklace.

They have called man little world.
What do they call woman then?
They should call her little heaven.

World   [*Speaks*] She has not read Ezekiel, who says
Pride turns beauty to ugliness.

Voice   [*Sings to Tune E*]
Human Beauty is a flower
And at nightfall it will wither.

Beauty   [*Speaks*]
A sad voice sings: Beauty must pass away.
Oh don't let Beauty die.
Let Beauty return to her first brightness
When she smiled like the dawn to see the dawn.
But there's no rose in all the world
Can open up her petals to
The golden flattery of the sun
Without those petals withering a little.
Once the green bud is open to the sky,
The green bud never closes.
But why should I care if the sun's red rays
Wrinkle the bright white flowers of dawn?
For I am an everlasting flower.
Though the sun saw me born in beauty,
It shall not see my death.
I'm told I'm eternal, so how can I die?
Sad voice, give me your reply.

Voice   [*Sings to Tune E*]
You have an eternal soul
But your body is a flower.
Like a flower it must die
And the time to go is now.

Beauty   [*Speaks*]
I can't argue with you. Although
I came in through the cradle, to the grave I go.
I would like to say before leaving this place,
I wish I'd played my part with better grace.

[*Exit* BEAUTY]

World   She ended well, with a repentant mind.

Rich Man   Beauty has gone away and left behind
All of her silks and fine array.
Beauty, beauty has gone away.

Peasant	If I get bread and wine and meat And a suckling pig to eat When next Easter comes around I shall miss Beauty, I'll be bound.
Beggar	I feel sorry for her. What shall we do?
Rich Man	We can talk and say what we think is true.
Peasant	[*Sings to Tune F*] When I think about the work I've done, Working in the rain and in the sun – My work Stole away my life. While I laboured at my working role I forgot to cultivate my soul. My soul. It was half-alive.
Voice	[*Sings to Tune F*] Peasant, now your work is at an end. You must labour in another land, A land Where you'll work for God.
Peasant	[*Speaks*] Voice, I want to appeal, let me appeal. I appeal to a higher court. Don't let me die just yet. Put it off till I've brought the crops in, I'd like to leave everything right. And I want to appeal, because, as you know, I've not been a good peasant. The thistles and weeds have grown so tall You can't tell my cornfields from my vineyards. My neighbour's barley grows giant-high, My crop wouldn't even hide a dwarf. My seeds just don't seem to want to grow. You may say, that's a good time to die, When your crops are bad, but what I say Is: by your fruit shall you judge them, right? Well my poor orchard is bare as a barrel. I'm not trying to be funny, Lord. Thank you very much for everything. I feel as if I'm dying now And the grave is yawning to swallow me up.

If I didn't quite get my part off pat
I'm sorry I'm not sorry about that.

[*Exit* PEASANT]

World   He was rather vulgar, our peasant friend,
But he certainly made an excellent end.

Rich Man   The Peasant has left behind his sweat,
His tools and his plough.

Beggar   We should not forget.
I weep for him. But what can we do?

Rich Man   We can talk, and say what we think is true.

[*Sings to Tune D*]
Since life's a rose that withers on the stem,
Let's raise the flask and drink it dry.
To loins and stomach, let's make gods of them!
Today we'll feast, tomorrow we must die.

World   Who is the next philosopher?

Beggar   I am – pay attention, sir.
[*Sings to Tune Q*]
O damn the day when I was born
And damn the night when I was conceived
To live in agony.
O let the sun be hidden away,
Fill all the air with darkness.
Let darkness rule and never be conquered,
So planet Earth is hidden from Heaven,
So I can be hidden, yes, hidden away.
[*Speaks*]
Lord, I don't despair because of the state I'm in
But because I was born in a state of sin.

Voice   [*Sings to Tune Q*]
Both joy and pain have days that are numbered,
So bring your accounts now, of both pain and joy.

Rich Man   Oh no!

Beggar   Good news!

Rich Man   Don't you want to run?

Beggar   Yes, I do.

Rich Man   Why not?

Beggar	It couldn't be done.

Beggar

                              It couldn't be done.
What's trembling is this soul of mine —
It's the natural fear of the Divine.
God's God — and that is frightening.
Can't you see it would be a futile thing
If a beggarwoman should try to flee?
The King could find no sanctuary
And Beauty no hiding place, and so
Where could poverty possibly go?
Rather I greet death as a friend
For now my life and my pain shall end.
Soon I shall be let out of my cage.

Rich Man   But aren't you sorry to quit the stage?

Beggar   I had no joy there, I go willingly.

Rich Man   My heart is left with my property.

Beggar   Joy.

Rich Man   Sorrow.

Beggar   Comfort.

Rich Man   Distress.

Beggar   Good luck.

Rich Man   Misery.

Beggar   Happiness.

               [*Exit* RICH MAN *and* BEGGAR]

Director   Soon you shall see how I reward
                        Those who acted well for the Lord
                        And you will see bad actors sent
                        To a place of punishment.

World   But before our modest play
                        Presents you a vision of Judgement Day,
                        Let our performing troupe intrude
                        To bring you a cheerful interlude.

               [*Interlude*]

               [*A Dance of Death in which the actors, in skeleton costumes, walk on bony stilts, juggle with skulls, enact weddings between skeletons etc.*]

Part Two

[*Enter the* WORLD]

World [*To Audience*]
Welcome back – you may have thought
Our play was brief – well, life is short,
Especially when you realise you've got
One entrance and one exit – that's your lot.
Now I collect and return to my store
The props they used and the costumes they wore,
Back to my cupboards they must go
For they were only used for show.
I shall stand here so I can make sure
They smuggle no finery out of that door.
They'll be swept off the stage, as we all must
Eventually be, in the form of dust.

[*Enter* KING]

Remind me, please. Could you just say
Which part you acted in the play?

King Has the world so quickly forgotten the King?

World The world, my friend, forgets everything.

King I was the diamond, the brilliant one,
Master of every land under the sun.
My crown and robes were of living light,
But now I lie in the arms of night.
I commanded, I judged, I achieved great renown,
I explored, I improved, I put enemies down,
I had prudent affairs, I possessed, I enjoyed,
I inherited wealth and I also employed
Thousands of courtiers, servants and cooks
And I wrote three ingenious history books.
You should have seen me when I sat alone
In my golden crown on my golden throne.

World Well, take off your crown, take it off, let it be.
Take off your robes and your memory.

[WORLD *takes robes and crown from* KING]

Nakedly exit from life's farce.
Your throne shall be filled by another's arse.

King	You gave me all that finery. Why do you grab it back from me?
World	I never gave you a single thing. The costume was lent while you played the King. I'll put your robes and crown over there For the next one who acts a King to wear.
King	What possible use has it been to me To have played a King of majesty?
World	Soon you will meet our Director Lord And receive your punishment or reward, Depending on whether you acted well Or badly. No, I couldn't tell, It's not my job to judge you here – But I am responsible for all this gear.

[*Enter* BEAUTY]

World	What part did you play?
Beauty	Human beauty.
World	What did I give you?
Beauty	Perfect beauty.
World	Where is it now?
Beauty	It stayed down in the grave.
World	All nature marvels, all nature sighs Seeing how rapidly Beauty flies. You cannot call her back across the years. When Beauty leaves, she simply disappears. She flies out of your arms on melting wings. I can collect the power which was the King's, But Beauty can't be kept in my store. Look in your mirror.
Beauty	I already saw.
World	Where are your elegance and loveliness? Try to return them like a borrowed dress!
Beauty	[*Sings to Tune O*] They are rotting in my coffin, They are crumbling, My roses in the grave, Lilies in the grave.

My ivory and crystal,
All my warmth and beauty.
  All my lovely plans,
  All my lovely thoughts,
  Broken in the grave.

[*Enter* PEASANT]

World   Yokel, come here. What was your part?

Peasant   Just a peasant, worth a spit and a fart
To the likes of you, who pompously tell
Us we're agricultural personnel.
I'm the kind whom courtiers put down
With names like clodhopper and clown,
Curmudgeon, chawbacon, churl and boor,
Bumpkin, yokel and many more
But they usually call us those names, I've found,
When they imagine that we're not around.
When they know I'm somewhere about the place
I'm "Him Over There" or "You With The Face."

World   Leave what I gave you to do the job.

Peasant   What did you ever give me, snob?

World   I gave you a hoe.

Peasant   You gave me a hoe?

World   You must hand it back, it's a debt you owe.

Peasant   Now my heart breaks, for I must go
Out of this hard world without my hoe
With which I had hoped to perform great deeds
Against the afterlife's thistles and weeds.

[*Enter the* RICH MAN *and the* BEGGAR]

World   Who's that?

Rich Man   One who wishes to stay with you always.

Beggar   And one who wished to be rid of you always.

World   Why these two attitudes to me?

Rich Man   I was rich as cream.

Beggar   I was poor as a flea.

World   Give up your jewels.
          [*Takes* RICH MAN*'s jewels*]

Beggar	What good luck! I find Without any regrets I leave the world behind.

[*Enter* CHILD]

World	You came to the theatre to act – so pray, Why did you not appear in the play?
Child	You took my life from me in the womb. There I leave all you gave me, in that tomb.
King	If only I'd spilt less blood in war!
Beauty	If only I'd spent less time at mirrors!
Rich Man	If only fewer possessions had owned me!
Peasant	If only I'd worked just one more Springtime!
Beggar	If only I had suffered more!
World	Too late now for If Only speeches. In the midwinter don't look for peaches. Now I've collected from his Majesty And frustrated the Rich Man's vanity. Now Beauty has seen where Beauty goes And sceptres are the same price as hoes – Come along with me, for we must leave This great stage of make-believe For the stage of Truth.
King	World, tell me why Are your greetings so different from your goodbye?
World	When a man receives something, food or alms, He extends his hands with open palms. When he wants to reject, he gives emphasis By turning them over, see, like this. This is the cradle, shaped to receive. This is the grave by which you must leave. I greeted you as a cradle might, But as your grave I must say goodnight.
Beggar	Let's find that great supper which our Lord Director offered for our reward.
King	Beggar, don't push in front of me. I'm the King! Have you lost your memory?
Beggar	What you were doesn't matter. Beyond the tomb All actors are equal in the dressing-room.

Rich Man	Remember you begged from me yesterday.
Beggar	Remember that you gave nothing away.
Beauty	Don't forget that you owe me the highest esteem, For I was more beautiful than a dream.
Beggar	Wealth and poverty, youth and age – We all look alike in our shrouds backstage.
Rich Man	Step aside, Peasant.

Peasant
                                    Now you are
Less than the shadow of a star.

Rich Man	The Director's eyes – they are frightening me.
Beggar	Director, the whole of your company Which acted in that little play Called Human Life, has come to say: Where's the great supper you said would be shared? May we see the Table? Is it all prepared?

[*The* DIRECTOR, *seated at his table, is revealed*]

Director	My table's ready with bread and wine On which all Heaven delights to dine. But I must know which of my company Shall ascend to my table to eat with me. For those who did not act their parts With their understanding and their hearts Shall not be seated. Let the Beggar stand. Come, sit with me, at my right hand. We shall dine together on Heaven's bread And your dear soul shall be comforted.

[BEGGAR *goes up and joins* DIRECTOR]

Beggar	Now I am blessed beyond belief. Now I wish I could have suffered more grief, For pain in the cause of godliness Does hurt, but it also brings happiness.
King	I humbly ask to be forgiven. Tell me, have I no hope of Heaven?
Director	Beauty and Majesty both lamented Their vanity. Since they repented They will come to this feast of mine When the Peasant comes to dine.

	[*To* BEGGAR] The Peasant spoke to you insultingly,
	But he gave you some bread, rather grudgingly.
Peasant	She fell in the trap of the layabout –
	I tried to provoke her to haul herself out.
Director	And you wept for your sins. And so all three
	Shall approach my table through Purgatory,
	That great expanse of time and space,
	That terrible desert, that torture place.
Beggar	The King gave me his hand, let me offer him mine.
	Let me help him up to your table to dine.

[BEGGAR *gives her hand to the* KING *and helps him up*]

Director	I remit the sentence which was your due.
	The Beggar has interceded for you.
Child	If I made no mistakes, good Lord,
	Why do I get no reward?
Director	You could hardly claim that you did well.
	You go neither to Heaven nor to Hell.
	You shall feel nothing, you shall be taken
	To limbo with pagans and the forsaken.
Child	Now I dream I am held tight
	In the arms of dreadful night.
Rich Man	Beauty and the King both shake.
	And I tremble like an earthquake.
	There's nowhere to hide. Though I expect a
	Hard judgment I must speak. Director!
Director	You are calling me? Have you no shame?
	You're right to shiver when you use my name.
	Rich Man, you shall no longer be
	An actor in my company.
	Go down to Hell where your love of gain
	Shall torture you with endless pain.
Rich Man	Help! Wrapped up in a flaming gown,
	Chained in shadows, I'm falling down,
	To a blind black room where I'll lie evermore
	On a rack of rock on a fiery floor.
Beggar	Infinite glory fills me now.
Beauty	I shall enjoy it some day, somehow.

Peasant	This is my treasured hope as well.
Rich Man	There is no treasure for us in Hell.
Director	See the Four Last Things. All things must end. Let Beauty and the Peasant Now ascend. The pair of them shall dine with me. They've earned their joy through agony. [BEAUTY *and the* PEASANT *go up and join the feast*]
Beauty	Happiness!
Beggar	Radiance!
Peasant	Consolation!
King	True victory!
Rich Man	Poisonous desolation!
Director	Angels in Heaven, the Devil in Hell, Humankind on earth and the beasts as well Prostrate themselves before this bread. So let the living and the dead And those who still await their birth Unite in Heaven, Hell and Earth To make the whole universe ring As every voice combines to sing.
	[*Shawms play and many voices sing the "Tantum Ergo"*]
World	And since this life is all a play, We hope, dear people, that we may Receive your applause for the way we played And pardon for all the mistakes we made.
	[*End*]